Guía de hoy
Barcelona
English

W0008532

ANAYA
TOURING

GUÍAS DE HOY
BARCELONA

Texts: **José María Carandell, José Ángel Cilleruelo, José Manuel Rafí, Josep Maria Canela, Juan Rosás, Guillermina Botaya**
and ANAYA/*touring* editorial team.
Translation: **James Cerne.**

Editorial Director: **Pedro Pardo.** Series Editor: **Mercedes de Castro.** Copy Editor: **Luis Daniel Fernández.** Maps: Cartografía ANAYA/*touring.* Photographic Researching and Editing: **José María Marcelino.** Technical Coordinator: **Antonio Martín.** Layout: **Alejandra Navarro** and **Silvia Jimeno.**

Photographs: **A.G.E.:** 132. **Aisa:** 24, 72, 86, 100, 121, 124. **Archivo Anaya:** 23, 25, 26, 27, 28, 29, 30, 112, 113, 128. **A. Martínez Bermejo:** 114. **F. Poo Egea:** 44, 51, 62, 66, 69, 93, 95, 101, 102, 103. **Index:** 47, 56 (upp/low), 63, 67, 68, 96, 97, 117. **Incafo:** 20, 41, 73, 90, 108 (right). **J. Gual:** 15, 22, 33, 61, 89, 108 (left). **M. Raurich:** Cover, 6, 7, 8, 11, 12, 19, 42, 45, 46, 55, 57, 59, 71, 76, 77, 80, 83 (low), 84, 87, 88, 105, 111, 119, 126, 129, 130, 131. **Paisajes Españoles:** 31, 79. **Sobremesa:** 110. **The Image Bank:** 16, 32, 35, 40, 43, 49 (low), 75, 81, 99. **Vision Agency:** 14, 49 (upp), 50, 60, 64, 65, 83 (upp), 85, 91, 104, 106, 127 (upp/low).

Production: **Antonio Mora** and **César Encinas.**

Cover and graphic designer: **José María Cerezo.**

Color separation: **Datacolor**

Printer: **Nuevo Servicio Gráfico Ibérico, S. A.** Binder: **Tudela, S. A.**

© Grupo Anaya, S. A., 1992
  Telémaco, 43. 28027 Madrid.

Depósito Legal: M - 44279 - 1991
I.S.B.N: 84 - 207 - 4388 - 7
Impreso en España - Printed in Spain

GENERAL INDEX

HOW TO USE THIS GUIDE

Before your trip

We suggest that you read the first part of this guide entitled **Impressions of Barcelona** (pages 7 to 31); articles on the nature of the people of the province, their history and art, written by José María Carandell. For those who believe that discovering the local food is one good reason for traveling, the section on *gastronomy* (pages 134 to 139) contains an overview of the specialities of Barcelona, which may whet your appetite.

During the trip

In the part entitled **Visit to the City of Barcelona** (from page 34 to 119), various itineraries through the city are described, where detailed information is given about each of the places of greatest interest.

In the section **Excursions from Barcelona** (from page 120 to 131), various side-trips are described, offering alternatives for visiting those places or landscapes which are of unique historic interest.

Time to eat

In the section entitled **What to do** you will find information about the location, quality and price of a wide variety of restaurants.

Entertainment

Also in the **What to do** section, you will find information about a good number of activities to help you spend your free time, ranging from local fiestas, to sports, shopping, shows...

Use the index

Finally, there is a list of place names, sights and spots of interest which will help you locate the pages containing pertinent information.

PLANNING YOUR TRIP

Depending on the time you have available, whether it be a few hours, a weekend, or a week or more, you will be able to get the most out of it by following these suggestions:

One week

Visit the city of Barcelona by following the itineraries proposed in the Guide. From the excursions through the province, choose the ones that most appeal to you. For your meals, follow the suggestions offered in the **Gastronomy** and **Restaurants** sections. If you are looking for some activity with which to occupy your leisure moments, consult the section **What to do.**

A Weekend

If you do not wish to leave the city of Barcelona, just follow the recommended itineraries. If you would like to explore further, choose from the number of appealing excursions through the province, but do so after having followed the Basic Itinerary through the city. The list of restaurants in the Guide will be helpful to you at mealtimes.

A few Hours

If you are just passing through the capital and only have a few hours available, take a walk through the city before having a meal in one of the restaurants indicated on pages 139 to 144.

Impressions of Barcelona
its history, people and landscapes

José María Carandell (Impressions). José Manuel Rafí and Josep Maria Canela (History)

A desire to stroll along the Ramblas, see the imaginative architectural works of Gaudí, or visit to the site of the 1992 Olympics might be what inspires you to come to Barcelona. Once in the city you will find more and more reasons to enjoy your stay, such as the vestiges of two thousand years of history, the city's urban layout or its extraordinarily dynamic citizens.

Modernist-style architecture has made a lasting contribution to Barcelona's decoration, especially through the buildings located in El Eixample.

A human river

The Rambla of all Ramblas

THE GOVERNMENT of the city of Barcelona wrote a letter in Catalan to King Alfonso IV (who was in Naples at the time) in the year 1444, to tell him of the successful completion of the construction of the upper part of the street La Rambla. For the previous century it had been merely an esplanade beside the city wall. After writing that the street was "beautiful and spacious" the governors added that "the citizens and inhabitants of the city, both men and women, and principally the common people, take their Sunday and holiday strolls on the street, in the summer as well as winter". In this oldest surviving written description of La Rambla you can recognize the street as it is today, the most pleasant place to have a stroll in Barcelona, for people of all kinds.

However, the last and final building was not complete on the whole length of La Rambla until the XVIII century, when, in imitation of the French boulevard, the pavement for the pedestrians was put in the centre, the lanes for wheeled traffic on the sides, and shade trees, mainly plane trees, were planted. Its success was such that it was soon imitated in other neighbourhoods in Barcelona, and in other cities in Catalonia.

The word "rambla" comes from the Arabic, and means "torrent", that is, a river bed that only occasionally has water flowing in it, usually in the autumn, in the rainy season. Although it is commonly believed that La Rambla was a torrent, it actually never was, even though one did pass by very near and parallel to it. In any case, La Rambla does have some characteristics of a river; its different widths, its curving layout over its 2 kilometre course, and it does receive human currents from the entire city and from the most diverse and distant origins. In La Rambla, these currents mingle. When strangers come to Barcelona, the first thing they usually visit is La Rambla, where they have a drink of water at the

❖
It is always enjoyable to stroll along Las Ramblas, and even more so when the morning is sunny and the atmosphere inviting.

fountain Fuente de Canaletes, water from the river of La Rambla, as tradition would have it.

going up from the port, La Rambla is divided into several parts, also known as "Ramblas", and two small squares, known as "Llano" or "Pla" (flatland). Here you have a list of their names; Rambla de Santa Mònica, Llano del Teatro, Rambla del Centro, Llano de la Boqueria, Rambla de San José, Rambla de los Estudios and Rambla de Canaletes. Recently La Rambla was lengthened around the west end of the Plaza de Cataluña, to connect it with the Rambla de Cataluña that crosses the new part of the city, even though they are very different, the one from the other.

La Rambla is equally appealing because of the people who stroll there, or are just passing through, or resting, looking, playing or performing; also because of its flower stalls, and the bird and small animal sellers; its benches and chairs, its shoe-shine boys; because of its fountains; book, magazine and newspaper kiosks, and the terraces of the bars; and because of its buildings, generally from the nineteenth century, but with some older ones (Gothic, Barroque and Neoclassic), some modernist houses and shops, and some twentieth-century buildings. Stroll slowly along it if you wish to see everything.

On the Rambla de Santa Mònica are the buildings of the Gobierno Militar; the recently restored Antigua Fábrica de Cañones; the Gothic Iglesia de Santa Mònica, now a centre for art expositions; the wax museum Museo de la Cera; and the Neoclassic Casa March, which houses the Consejería de Cultura de la Generalitat. In the Plaza del Teatro is the Teatro Principal, from the xvi century, today the property of Liceu, and across from it, the monument to the Catalan playwright Pitarra. The now much-frequented stately porticos of the Plaza Real distinguish the Rambla de los Capuchinos (also called "Rambla del Centro"). There you find the Hotel Cuatro Naciones, a favourite of the men and women from the Romantic period, such as George Sand, Chopin and Liszt; and the Hotel Orient, where Anderson stayed; and the Gran Teatro de Liceu, dedicated to opera and ballet performances.

❖ *El Mercado de la Boqueria is the most popular and prestigious of the City of the Count; doubtlessly because of both the quality and selection of its produce, as well as its splendid display.*

The Llano de la Boqueria has always been a central meeting point for people of the city; it has a mosaic by Joan Miró (who was born near-by) in its pavement. What most sets the Rambla de las Flores apart, besides its flower-sellers, is its Mercado de la Boqueria, with its shouting, smells and colours; and its Barroque Palacio de la Virreina, presently the headquarters of the Consejería de Cultura del Ayuntamiento and exposition hall. The Iglesia de los Jesuitas, and the Academia de Ciencias y Artes, where the Teatro Poliorama is, are the most interesting features of the Rambla de los Estudios, with its Palacio Moja, which belonged to the Comillas family, and where Cinto Verdaguer lived. It is today the seat of the Consejería de Cultura de la Generalitat. Finally, although the Rambla de Canaletes lacks the interesting buildings of the other parts, its history is no less eventful. For example, it was the site of the University, and the famous nationalist revolt of *els segadors* began here against Felipe IV.

The people of Barcelona call this main prom-enade either La Rambla or Las Ramblas, even though they know it is officially called "La Rambla". ◆

Catalan Modernism

Gaudí, the Great Genius

I T SEEMS no exageration to say that Antoni Gaudí was the most creative and original Catalan artist. He was born in Reus in 1852. At that time Reus was second only to Barcelona in size. Two other people, the painter Mariano Fortuny and the politician General Prim, who were important to Catalonia and to Spain, were also born there in the nineteenth century. Gaudí spent his childhood in his parents' workshop (they were boilermakers) and the fields of Riudums, near Reus, in the family's country home. Gaudí learned to appreciate the volume of the boilers in the workshop, something that would later influence his conception of buildings as sculptures. In the country he learned to love the great outdoors; a great part of his work is a paean to a rustic, natural world. As a child he was shy and kept to himself; he was frightened of girls; in fact he never managed to get married, and his love affairs never passed beyond a stage of platonic dreaming, as far as we know. There is some evidence that when he was studying architecture (thanks to the patronage of a gentleman of Reus) his life was more or less carefree for a time, and he got to know some prostitutes; but according to all the anecdotal evidence he seems to have been rather aggresive in his relations with women. Thus the wife of his grand maecenas and friend, the Count of Güell, referred to him disparagingly as "that López"; when a woman told him that her piano no longer fit in the house that he had just finished fixing for her, the architect replied, "Play the violin, Madame". He was always squabbling with Doña Rosario Segimon, for whom he built one of his best buildings, La Pedrera. Whereas, he cultivated great friendships with men; with the above-mentioned Güell, and his many collaborating architects, who respected him greatly, even though he did tend to remain somewhat aloof.

Once his period of apprenticeship and his first works were completed, Gaudí threw himself

❖

Park Güell is an urban environment where art and nature have been successfully integrated, through the use of rustic materials, in cases such as the one shown in the photograph on the left.

into architecture with daring zeal and liberty, creating works that were not just notably original but also representative of Modernist architecture, a style that was born, in large measure, thanks to his efforts. He was responsible for a few works outside of Catalonia, such as the house El Capricho in Comillas; the Episcopal Palace of Astorga, and the house of the Botine family in León; but his great works are in Barcelona. Here you find the Casa Vicens, the Teresianas school, the Casa Bellesguard, the Palacio Güell, the Casa Batlló, La Pedrera, the Parc Güell and Church of the Sagrada Familia, among others. As one of his most highly creative works, the crypt of the Colonia Güell deserves special mention; it is in Sant Coloma de Cervelló, a town outside of Barcelona. His construction innovations stand out in all of these works, a product of his deep knowledge of geometry, a study that absorbed him from his childhood on. He also had a deep understanding of the different construction techniques then in existence, from the humblest to the most complex, although he systematically avoided the technological innovations of his day, being basically anti-industrialist by temperament. He preferred to work with stone, ceramic tile, wood and wrought iron.

His imaginative inventions also stand out, perhaps even more, both in each of his buildings (which are matchless, unique works of art) and

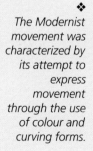

❖

The Modernist movement was characterized by its attempt to express movement through the use of colour and curving forms.

in the details, which he studied with as much attention as the overall work, without ever losing sight of the wishes of his clients; the function to which the work was to be dedicated; his artistic creativity; a certain conception of the world, the fruit of his ideas and experiences, of a symbolic character; and the glory of God. Of the nearly one hundred architects and master builders who created modernism, above all in Catalonia, but also in Valencia, Majorca, Galicia and other places in Spain, Gaudí is the one who shines most, due to his genius, comparable with those other few great creators of his time in the world. But in Barcelona there were other Modernist architects of considerable interest, such as Josep María Jujol, who began with Gaudí as a youth, and who produced works of notable originality; or Lluis Domenach i Montaner, more rational and liberal in his art than Gaudí, who produced works of the calibre and richness of the Palau de la Musica Catalana, the Casa Lleó Morera, the Casa Navas and the Hospital de San Pablo: and finally, Josep Puig i Catalfach, who was a politician and President of the Mancomunidad de Catalunya, and a great specialist in medieval European art, besides being the architect responsible for such buildings as the Casa Amatller and the Casa de les Punxes, among many others.

❖
A detail of Park Güell, with its new iconography and innovative techniques.

But Catalan Modernism was not confined to architecture. In it there was something of everything; the paintings of Rusiñol, Casas, Mir and Nonell; the sculpture of Llimona; the music of Morera; the writing of Maragall, Puig i Ferrater and Víctor Català; cultural movements such as that which produced the magazine *L'Avenç*. There was even a completely deliberate Modernist style of clothing and customs at that time. And in addition to all of that, there was the Modernism of the arts related with architecture, such as interior decorating, furnture making, stained glass, stuccos, mural painting, pottery for different uses, and wrought-iron work. Even more, the style was not evinced in houses alone, but also in the churches, in cafés, in pharmacies and all types of shops.　　　◆

The New Barcelona

The Four Corners of the Olympic Games

WHEN BARCELONA was chosen as the site of the 1992 Olympic Games, there was at first great euphoria in the city, as if the people had been awaiting this prize for years and years. But soon a kind of stupor set in, the source of which was evidently a fear that the city could not be got ready for such an important international event. The traditional Spanish lack of confidence in their own abilities was projected in the form of jokes about the incompetence of the project leaders. That is why the people began talking of failure when the Olympic Ring project was announced; its initial difficulties were taken to be the confirmation of the validity of their first dark forbodings. When two years had passed, the first half of the construction period, people began to understand that the large sums of money involved were really being generated in the city and the nation, and that the work was actually going ahead. The Olympic buildings began to rise up from within the older, traditional urban landscape. Two years ago, or decades, or a century ago, the city was not so self-confident as it is now.

Although it would be wonderful for Barcelona, Catalonia and Spain to earn gold medals in the Olympics, first and foremost for the city is to obtain the Olympic title for its four corners, which may seem an easy task, but is more serious than one might imagine, given the world importance and international repercussions of the event.

Parallel to this increase in self-confidence, people are beginning to conceive of the city in a new way, discovering new zones and new perspectives, thrown into relief by the Olympic construction projects. Thus, people began to understand that Barcelona is not an old city surrounded by modern buildings, but is like a game board where some zones are almost completely isolated from others. The Olympic

❖

The Fabra Observatory on Tibidabo seems to spend its days contemplating the huge city that sprawls out from its base to the sea.

projects will put an end to this isolation within the city.

The shape of Barcelona is roughly rectangular, with the Sierra de Collserola and Tibadabo above it, the sea below, the Besós River to the north and the Llobregat River to the south. And the installations of the Olympic Games are being built to occupy the four corners of this rectangle, approximately.

The main area, the Anillo Olimpico (Olympic Ring), is on the mountain of Montjuïc; the Olympic Village, first for the use of the atheletes, then later for those who have bought the flats, as well as the Olympic harbour, are in the industrial and workers' area of Pueblo Nuevo; the area of F.C. Barcelona, for the soccer matches, is in the well-known middle class zone of Pedralbes; and the area of El Valle de Hebrón is dedicated to various competitions, the housing for journalists and referees.

Some very architecturally important urban works have been inspired by the Olympic Games. Of course, the main ones are those of the Anillo Olimpico in Montjuïc, whose prinicpal building is the newly built Stadium. The façade of the old stadium was kept, out of respect for traditional values, so they say. The tradition itself may be of arguable associations, as the old stadium was, for many years, the home of the unfortunate ones who found themselves otherwise homeless. But however the old stadium was, the place where the Olympic Games are to be held is certainly going to be fine.

The other grand ediface is the Palace of Sant Jordi (Palacio de Sant Jordi), perhaps of all the buildings the most interesting, from an architect's point of view, and certainly the most technically innovative. Its author, the Japonese architect Arata Isozoki, said during its inauguration that he would be really pleased if people would begin to call his building for sporting events and musical concerts the "beatle". It seems that he had this beautiful, primitively lovable creature of the mountain in his mind's eye when he conceived of this stadium covered with a strong, shining carapace, dotted with little bull's-eye windows.

❖
The gigantic buildings of the Hotel Arts and Torre Mapfre rise up like olympic watchmen on the shore of the legendary Mare Nostrum.

The third important construction project is the Sports University, Universidad del Deporte (INEF), work of the always controversial Ricardo Bofill, which might be called Postmodern in style, due to its ironic use of the classic style.

And finally, there is the Olympic Village, called Nueva Icaria to comemmorate a utopic socialist experiment which was very popular in this area, previously full of factories and workers' homes.

It is the project which has inspired the greatest hopes, since it is a completely new quarter, of considerable quality, beside the sea. Outstanding in it are two skyscrapers which seem to signal to those who arrive at the city of Barcelona by ship.

There is also the Olympic water sports harbour, the road network of motorways, pedestrian streets and avenues, the shopping centre, park and gardens and the area of homes. The buildings are mainly interesting due to their up-to-date services and facilities; and due to their artistic merit, for they were designed by the best Catalan architects.

But there are so many other construction projects that one could say that Barcelona will be fundametally different after the Olympics have ended, as the city moves on to the end of the twentieth century. ◆

Barcelona, Two-thousand Year Old City

ON OCTOBER 2, 1988 the Mayor of Barcelona was presented with the Olympic flag in the city of Seul, Korea. Thus began what will finish in the summer of 1992, with the celebration of the Olympic Games of the XXV Olympics.

The desire of the city's folk to host the Olympics is not new nor a whim, since the role of games-host was solicited unsuccessfully five times before. As an anecdote, a citizen of the Roman *Barcino* won the quadriga race in the Helenic Olympics of the year 229. Other events have occurred which demonstrate this open talent of the city; on May 20, 1888 (a year before the expositon was held in Paris), Queen María Cristina, the widow of Alfonso XII, inaugurated the first Exposición Universal in the Parc de la Ciutadella. Construction projects from that event left the monument to Christopher Columbus, the Paseo de Colón, La Ramble de Catalunya and the Arc de Triomf on the Passeig de Sant Joan, which in its day was used as the entrance to the fairgrounds. Years later, in June of 1929, Barcelona held another Exposición Universal, that time housed within the area of Montjuïc. On that occasion they built on the lands of the Plaça Espanya, the y put up the fountain Font Màgica, by Carles Buigas, the Palau Nacional (today the museum of Roman and Greek art), "El Poble Espanyol" and the stadium that in 1992, remodled inside, will be the site of the principal ceremonies of the Olympic Games.

These are signs of a will to live, of a city that has not stopped growing since it was founded two thousand years ago.

And although legend vinculates the city's birth with a mythological being (as do the legends of all cities that have a good opinion of themselves), in particular with the voyage of Hercules in his search for the golden apples; or with the noble family of the Barca, from Carthage (do not forget about Hannibal and Hamilcar), the truth seems to be that, in spite of the many

❖
Barcelona's past splendour, in the Middle Ages, left many notable examples of Gothic art in the city.

❖

*Funeral style in
the classic part
of Barcelona.*

findings from the Neolithic in different parts of
the city, the first signs of stable settlements come
from a tribe known as the "Laietanos", an Iberian tribe from the fifth century BC which inhabited the knolls that interrupt the plain between
the Llobregat and Besós Rivers. Contacts with
the Greeks led to the coining of money called
"Iberic Drachmas". Some of these coins found
in the plain bear the inscription *Laie,* others
Barkeno, probably the oldest reference to what
would become the name of the city.

After the Punic Wars, towards the year 48 BC,
the presence of the Romans becomes notice-
able. In the first century AD, the city was given
the official title of Colonia Iulia Augusta Paterna
Faventia Barcino. The traditional layout of the
city around an intersection of two avenues
whose crossing forms the Forum can still be
seen today. The Plaça de Sant Jaume was this
centre of politics; nearby you can see the
remains of the temple of Augusto (outside the
Centre Excursionista de Catalunya).

Curiously, here you see an example of the con-
tinuity of history, since this old centre of political
power is still today such a centre, as the City
Hall and headquarters of the regional government are located on this square.

The stretches of wall that you can see in the
Plaça de la Catedral belonged to the fortifications of the III and beginnings of the IV centuries,
after the first invasions, after Barcelona had
been the capital of the *Hispania Citerior,* replac-
ing *Tarraco* (Tarragona) in this role. The oldest
survivng historical reference to the city dates
from this period, from the book on the life of
San Jerónimo, from the year 392.

With the arrival of the Visigoths, Barcelona was
relagated to an unimportant role, although it
did recover some of its position as capital of the
kingdom for a few short months during the
reign of Autaúlfo, until he was killed by the
commander of his armies in 415. Between the
end of the VII century and the Arab conquest,
which the Medieval historian Ibn Idari placed
between 714 and 718, we know nothing of
events there. In any case, the domination of the
Moors was brief. In the year 801 the troops of

the Frank Ludovico Pío reconquered it and set up their capital of the Marca Hispánica. As it was a frontier city, its first count, Count Berá, had to withstand numerous attacks both from the Moors and the Visigoths discontent with the Frankish rule. The most famous of these attacks was the one by Almanzor in 985, which completely destroyed the city.

Count Borrell was the one responsible for the independence of his fiefdom of Barcelona from vassalage to the Franks in the time of Hugo Capeto. Thus was begun the formation of feudal Catalonia, with capital in Barcelona. From the x century until the union with the crown of Castille in the xv century, Barcelona experienced a period

❖

Greco-Roman mosaic that testifies to the presence of the classic civilizations in the old city of Barcino.

of tremendous political splendour as it expanded around the Mediterranean. At the beginning of the xi century, the growth of the population was such that the areas outside the walls near the churches and monasteries that were scattered over the plain, became places of permanent dwellings. It was the time of the Viles Noves (new towns), which produced such buildings of today as those near Santa Maria del Pi, Sant Pere de Puelles and the Jewish ghetto, Call Judío.

In the xii century the possessions of the Count of Barcelona were united to those of the Crown

Barcelona's maritime activity reached the peak of its splendour in the Middle Ages, but it has also continued strong and uninterrupted until our own times.

of Aragón, through the marriage of the Catalan Ramon Berenguer IV and Peronella, the daughter of the King of Aragón, Ramiro. In that century a series of different juridical norms were compiled in the book *Usatges de Barcelona*, which might be considered the oldest European constitution, In the year 1265, during the reign of Jaume I "el Conqueridor", the Consell de Cent was founded. It was a municipal government institution that represented all classes of citizens.

Another example of the early appearence of social norms in Barcelona is a legislative corpus, a collection of orders, customs and maritime habits that would later be imitated by many European cities. This legialative corpus was entitled *Llibre Apellat Consolat de Mar* (Book called Counsulate of the Sea), and its appearence coincided with the great expansion throughout the Mediterranean by the fleet from Barcelona. The Confederation of Catalonia-Aragón managed to dominate, during that period, Sardinia, Sicily, Malta, Naples, Albania, Corcega and the dukedoms of Athens and Neopatria, in Greece. There were also commercial consulates in all the major port cities of the *Mare Nostrum*.

The walls of Pere III are from this period. They were built to defend the Viles Noves and the Drassanes (shipyards, today made into a maritime museum). The royal palaces, Major and Menor, were built (of the later only the chapel is still standing) and the building of the Cathedral was begun. The guilds of that time left their names on some of the streets in the area where they worked *(frassaders, mirallers, cotoners...).* There was an outbreak of the Black Plague in 1374, and a period of general decline began. Another factor in the decline was the civil war against Joan II. Internal disagreements were heightened; the organs of municipal power became divided into those of the "Busca" (political representation of the craftsmen, merchants and poor) and the "Biga" (the opposed faction of the nobles and bourgiousie). There were constant battles between the two groups. The city's population was approximately 35,000 then.

The purely dynastic union with the kingdom of Castille brought with it municipal reform, where the political posts were filled according to a system of "insaculación" (designation by drawn lots of the municipal posts). It also brought Ferrán II and Isabel de Castilla, the "Catholic Monarchs", who set up their capital for a brief period in Barcelona. Ferrán was

❖
The exceptional Las Reials Drassanes testify to Barcelona's importance as a ship-building port in the Middle Ages.

wounded in an assaination attempt, and his convalescence required the capital to be moved. In April of 1493 the Monarchs welcomed Christopher Columbus here on his arrival from his first voyage to the American continent. At that time the city was home to large communities of Jews and people from Genova, Pisa and Egypt, source of its cosmopolitan spirit.

The growth of the power of Turkey made a confrontation with western Europe inevitable; in October of 1571 a Christian fleet set sail from the port of Barcelona, to fight and win the battle of Lepanto. The Admiral in charge was Lluís de Requesens. A reproduction of the flagship is in the Museo Marítimo, and its crucifix, with the legend of the miracle included, is exhibited in a chaple of the Cathedral. Miguel de Cervantes, who fought in this battle and lost an arm there, wrote in his *El Quijote* in 1615; "Barcelona, archive of courtesy, refuge of foreigners, homeland of the brave, revenge of the offended,

❖
On the feast day of Corpus Christi in 1640, Catalonia rebelled against the policies being carried out by the Conde-Duque.

pleasing response to firm friendship and located in a place of unique beauty...". In 1609 the Banc de la Ciutat was founded.

The policies of Count-Duke Olivares, the poor state of the economy of the country and other factors led to the so-called War dels Segadors in 1640. Luis XIII of France was proclaimed Count of the city of Barcelona, and on the hill of Montjuic a major battle was fought between royal troops and the Catalans. Pau Claris, Tamarit and Fontanella were some of the leaders of that time, whose names are comemmorated on some of the city streets. In 1652 Barcelona capitulated to the troops of Felipe IV, and the castle of Montjuic, built only a short time before, became a barracks for the Crown's troops. In 1657 a census indicated a populatioon of 64,000.

In the War of Succession to the Spanish Throne, the Consell de Cent supported the cause of Archduke Carlos, opposing Felipe V. The conflict began in 1705 and lasted until September 11, 1714, when Bourbon troops entered Barcelona from the villages of Sants and Les Corts (today neighbourhoods of the city) in their final attack. In remembrance of that event, the National Fiesta of Catalunya, La Diada, is celebrated.

❖
Portrait of the first Spanish Bourbon, King Felipe V.

In 1716, with the publication of the Decreto de Nueva Planta, the first Bourbon king proceded to radically transform and suppress the Corts Catalans, La Generalitat, the Consell de Cent and other governing institutions. The university was also taken out of the city of Barcelona, and moved to the village of Cervera. More than 800 houses were torn down in the neighbourhood of La Ribera to build a fortress designed to suppress possible future rebellions. The Dutchman Prosper de Verboom designed the military structure, which today is used by the citizens for their relaxation, in an extensive and beautiful park, the site of museums, a zoo and the Parlament de Catalunya.

After its defeat in 1714, Barcelona concentrated on its economic recovery. In 1756 the Reial Companyia de Comerç de Barcelona was established, and King Carlos III allowed Catalonia to participate in commerce with the Americas, which had been prohibited since its discovery in 1492. From 1774 on, the city walls began to be torn down and the charismatic, poular Ramblas were built. In 1792 the dean of newspapers, the *Diario de Barcelona* was founded (known as "el Brusi"), whose first issue reached the streets on

❖

It was at the end of the XVIII century that Barcelona's society became decidedly open and dynamic.

October 1. It is still being published today. At the end of that century there were 115,000 people living in Barcelona, and although the Napoleonic Wars decimated the population, the census of 1849 indicated a population of 175,331.

The nineteenth century was that of the Industrial Revolution. Steam power entered the factories of Bonaplata, inaugurated in Calle Tallers in 1813. City gas lighted the streets from 1826, and in 1848 the railroad joined the two cities of the state, Barcelona and Mataró, for the first time. In 1854 more of the city walls were torn down to make room for the growing popultation. The seconmd grand transformation of the the city, the one that was to give it its present-day apearence, came from the hand of the engineer Ildefons Cerdà (1816-1876), who in 1859 designed the reordering of the flatland of the Llobregat, as a place where Barcelona could spread out into. in 1860 Queen Isabel II inaugurated l'Eixample, as this new neighbourhood was called, and a short time later the poet Víctor Balaguer gave names to its streets and avenues to commemorate past glories and the men who had made history in the country. Towards the end of the century (1873) electricity arrived, to substitute for the gas street-lighting, and the city put on a modern face for the world in its exposition in 1888.

With the annexation by the city of the villages in the flatland (which continue to maintain their idiosyncrasies and particular fiestas; some people in these neighbourhoods still speak of "going down to Barcelona" when they mean going "downtown") such as Les Corts, Sant Gervasi, Gràcia, Sant Andreu de Palomar and Sants, the population reached 553,000, according to the census of 1900. The villages of Sarria and Horta were absorbed around 1921.

Perhaps all of these changes cannot be explained without referring to the cultural features that proportioned them. At the turn of the century there was a rebirth of the Catalan literature (a movement that was called "Renaix-

❖

In the xix century there was considerable social unrest, almost always put down by military might.

ença"), and afterward Modernism contributed enormously to the spread of the use of Catalan. There were writers such as Verdeguer, Maragall, Guimerà; and publishers such as Valentí Almirall, the creator of the first Catalan-language newspaper (1879); newspapers such as *La Vanguardia* (1881) and the *Correo Catalán* (1876); architects such as Gaudí, Domènech i Montaner, Puig i Cadalfach, whose works beautified the streets of the "Grand Barcelona", as they were so fond of calling it in those times.

In the tavern of the "Cuatre Gats", which is still

open for business today, Ramón Casas, Nonell, Apel les Mestres, Rusiñol and Picasso would meet to chat. Enric Granados and Isaac Albéniz composed their works; l'Orfeó Catala and the Cors de Clavé gave voice to the response of the man in the streets to these events. The new sport of football arrived, brought by the Swiss Joan Gamper; in 1899 the F.C. Barcelona was founded, and because of the large number of foreigners in it, the following year the "Societat Espanyola de Football", the future "R.C.D. Espanyol", was founded.

The turn of the century also brought conflicts and civic insecurity with it, as for example when a bomb exploded in 1893 in the Teatro de la Opera del Liceu, causing many casualties. To terminate that wave of terrorist attacks, whose lamentable culmination was the Semana Trágica of 1909, when several churches and convents were burned, Primo de Rivera became Dictator in 1923. The ensuing pacification allowed the Exposición Universal to be put on in 1929. One year later the census registered one million inhabitants. During the Second Republic the Estatut de Nuria was approved, and many Catalan institutions were returned to legal status. The Plaça de Sant Jaume, as on so many other occasiones, was the place where the news was broken to the poulation. Later came the three years of civil war. Barcelona was part of the Republican side, and the city was the scene of violent combat. After the end of the conflict the flow of immigrants from the south was continuous; many outlying neighbourhoods sprang up, where life was precarious. Spurred by an increase in the price of tram fare, popular unrest exploded into the often-recalled general strike of 1951, the first since the beginning of the regime of Franco.

In 1952, international recognition of the regime allowed the celebration in Barcelona of the Congreso Eucaristico Internacional. At that time the quarter of Camp de la Bota was rebuilt, part of the shanty towns were torn down, and the Barri del Congrés was put up. While Porcioles was Mayor (1957-1973), the municipal charter of 1961 was obtained, which allowed the city gov-

❖

Detail from a view of Barcelona in the xix century.

❖ *The renovated Olympic Stadium had to wait more than half a century to host the Olympic Games for which it was built.*

ernment greater autonomy. It will be remembered for its accompanying exorbitant real-estate speculation and its tremendous structual deficiencies. The high-speed belt roads were begun to be built during that period, as well as the airport of Prat del Llobregat, the central market (Mercabarna); and the Metropolitan Municipal Corporation was created.

With the arrival of democracy a socialist was elected Mayor. The ruling party sponsored construction projects of such squares as the Plaça dels Països Catalans, in Sants; and the restructuring of some neighbourhoods which had lacked major facilities, such as the Casc Antic and Gràcia. The choice was made for high-speed belt roads, with the construction of the motorway along the coast and the fast-access tunnels of Rovira and Tibidao. The census of 1986 indicated a population of nearly two million.

The hosting of the Olympic Games will radically transform Barcelona's urban structure. The construction of the Olympic Village, the new hotels, again the architectural design, and world attention that will be directed at the city during the ceremonial acts will make of Barcelona a modern, cosmopolitan city, faithful to its citizens and open to those strangers who would like to get to know it. ◆

Visit to the city and the excursions from Barcelona

José Ángel Cilleruelo and José María Carandell (boxes)

Although today all of them are known by the same name, the many cities that Barcelona has been over the course of history include the Roman one, defended by its rotund walls; the ancient city, Gothic and lordly; the geometric expansion in El Eixample; and the Barcelona of the Olympics, which in one decade has brought about changes that otherwise would have taken a century.

Vigorous urban expansion has given rise to the creation of squares such as that of l'Espanya Industrial. Above these lines, a taxi, which has become one of the city's symbols.

VISIT TO THE CITY OF BARCELONA

Barcelona, an attractive and important European city, visited each year by thousands of people, will always afford all those who come to it something new to discover.

The "City of the Count" (as it is also known) is situated in the northwestern part of the Iberian Peninsula, on the shore of Mare Nostrum; it is one of the main ports on the Mediterranean Sea. It is bounded on the north by the Besós River, and the Llobregat River on the south. On the west it is bounded by the Sierra de Collserola, and on the east by the sea.

It is an old city, one that enjoyed a period of splendour during the Middle Ages. A vestige of those times is the Berri Gotic (Gothic Quarter), where there are not only major architectural works, but also the street layout of the medieval city.

However, Barcelona has never been content to rest on its laurels; it has always been interested in change, looking for the modern, as the building of its Eixample quarter demonstrated in the middle of the last century, and its race against the clock in the preparation of the site for the XXV Olympic Games demonstrates today.

Barcelona is today the administrative capital of Catalonia and the seat of the parliament (Parlament) and government of its autonomous community (Generalitat), and without doubt one of the most dynamic and enterprising of cities, while still managing to be a charming place, full of rewarding corners worth visiting.

Planning your visit

Different itineraries are proposed in the following, as a means for visiting the City of the Count.

The **Basic Itinerary, Barrio Gótico** and **El Eixample** sections include the most important sights in Barcelona.

The tours through **Olympic Barcelona** and **Unique Quarters** will enable you to get to know the Olympic-Games part of the city, as well as other areas which are fundamental for a well-rounded view. There are two maps on pages 36, 37 and 38 to help you orient yourself and locate the places of interest. The Roman numeral, the letter and Arabic numeral will help you locate the sights on the map; for example **Iglesia del Betlem** (I, D1).

The asteriscs (* or **) refer to the item's importance or special interest, respectively.

Basic Itinerary

- ❖ Plaça Catalunya
- ❖ La Rambla
- ❖ Portal de la Pau
- ❖ Passeig Colom
- ❖ Passeig d'Isabel II and Pla del Palau
- ❖ Santa Maria del Mar
- ❖ Carrer Montcada
- ❖ Plaça Ramon Berenguer III and Plaça del Rei
- ❖ Plaça de Sant Jaume
- ❖ The Cathedral
- ❖ Plaça Nova
- ❖ Palau de la Música Catalana

❖Plaça Catalunya (I, C1)
The heart of a Spanish city is always its square, the place where roads meet and the main buildings are built, and where its citizens gather and live together. The heart of the old Barcelona was the Plaça de San Jaume, which the city government still keeps up. But from the beginnings of this century the role of meeting place, of both lives and roads, has been played by the Plaça de Catalunya, on the boundary of the old city (built within the walls during its many centuries of life), and at the same time the link with the new city, refounded in the nineteenth century on the basis of a geometric layout. Your visit in Barcelona will begin, then, in its present-day heart. The origin of the well-known square and of its name

The Plaça de Cataluya is the place where all the main streets come together, about which the lives of all the citizens revolve.

BARCELONA / II

BARCELONA / I

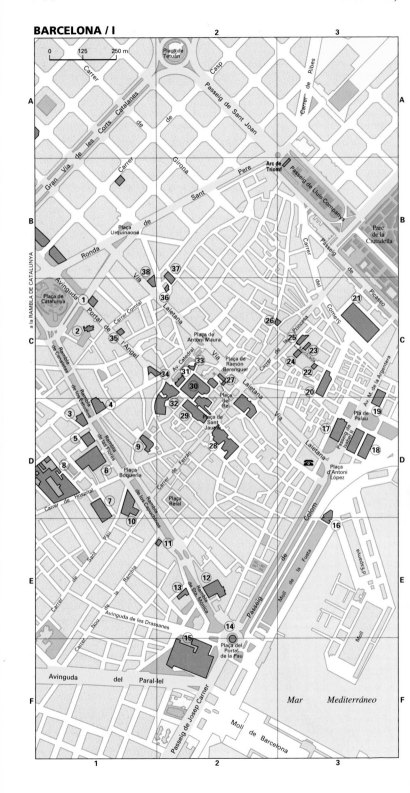

lies with the people. In the year 1848 a gate in the wall of the upper part of La Rambla was built, to facilitate access to some open, unused land. The people began using this land more and more on their strolls through the area. Once the walls were taken down, and plans were drawn up for the new neighbourhoods to be built there, no provision was made for such a grand square. But the people, used to strolling there, protested, and got the backing of the press in their demands for a public space. Several monumental projects were drawn up for the square during the time that one century ended and the next began, but the project was not definitely terminated until 1927. The architect Francesc Nebot (who also designed the façade of the **building** of the **Compañía Telefónica** on the same square in 1927) was responsible for the square's design. The circular space of the square includes an open central area, where children like to feed the pigeons, and the people of Barcelona meet; and a belt of gardens that culminate, in the higher part, in an ornamental group composed of two symetric fountains and a group of statues with the outstanding *Pastor tocant el flabiol* (a typical Catalan musical instrument) by Pau Gargallo (1881-1934), sculpted in the stone of Montjuïc. In the mosaic of the central part there is a sort of compass card which points out the directions peculiar to the city (mountain, sea, left and right), which do not correspond with the four cardenal points. Thus the sea-mountain axis passes through the city in a southeast-northwest direction.

The buildings that flank the square are of an eminently commercial function (banks, department stores, offices). Among them there are two Neogothic-style **houses** worthy of mention, one at the beginning of the Passeig de Gràcia, numbers 2 and 4, the project of Enric Sagnier (1855-1931), which dates from 1891; and the other at number 9 of the square, built one year later, designed by Joaquim Bassegoda (1854-1938). Both were restored with exemplary care in the past decade. On the neighbouring street Carrer Bergara, which runs into the west side of the square, at number 11 there is a third interesting **house,** also coming from the last century, which has a unique façade where wrought iron was made good use of.

Down a tiny passageway (Carrer Rivadeneyra) in the lower part of the square you can reach the **Monasterio de Santa Ana,** whose Romanesque church, founded in the XII century, has been preserved only two steps away from, and at the back of, the modern city centre. A little garden helps to protect the place from the hustle and bustle that surrounds it. The main door is Gothic (1300), and inside you can visit its cloister and chapter room.

❖ La Rambla (I, C1)

Two of the main roads which transect Barcelona meet in the Plaça de Catalunya. One of them, the Passeig de Gràcia, passes through the city's newer zone, and the other, La Rambla, through the old part. La Rambla is one of the places that is most representative of Barcelona. Even though it is somewhat longer than one kilometre, you can walk its entire length without crossing a street, or having to pay attention to the traffic. So you are free to stroll along and fix your attention in either the monumental buildings that flank it, or in the rich atmosphere provided by the people who flock there at all hours of the day or night.

Moreover, each one of the sections of La Rambla has its own particular character. Around Canaletas there are usually groups of men who get together spontaneously to speak about the local football clubs; a bit farther below on the walk are the bird-sellers' stalls with their song and colour; then there are the flower stalls with their fragrance and colour; next come the lively, jolly terraces; and on the final stretch there is an open-air crafts market every weekend.

Another attraction of La Rambla is its newspaper kiosks, over-

Everyone who would like to stroll once again down Las Ramblas, will doubtless do it if they drink the water of the unique Fuente de Canaletes.

flowing with publications from half the world, and open twenty-four hours a day.

Your planned itinerary consists of a tour divided into two parts, split so that you will be able to see the places of interest to both sides of the half-way point.

In its beginning La Rambla roughly corresponded with a geographical feature, the dry wash through which the waters from the neighbouring Collserola occasionally flowed down through the flatland. In fact, the Arabic word from which the word "rambla" (sandy place) comes gives a clear idea of its geographical origin. In the XIII century King Jaume I directed the builders of the medieval wall to take advantage of this dry wash in their defensive planning; thus La Rambla became part of the fortified enclave, from the Plaça de Catalunya to the Portal de Pau. In the XVI century the character of the zone changed, as it became a site for many new convents, monasteries and scholarly institutions.

Beginning in the XVIII century it became a place for the townspeople to take their constitutionals. This was especially true after the medieval wall was torn down in 1860. Since then it has gone on acquiring an increasingly healthier look, more and more life and activity.

The first stretch of La Rambla was given the name of Canaletes to commemorate a tower that was once part of the medieval wall. On its site there is today a **fountain** from the XIX century. Some would have it that

A typical view of Barcelona, on La Rambla de las Flores.

if you drink the waters of the fountain, you will find yourself ineluctably drawn to return to Barcelona in the future.

On your right, as you walk down, you will find the church **Iglesia de Betlem** (I, D1); its lateral façade gives onto La Rambla, although its main door opens onto the corner of Carrer del Carme. The church, with its single nave and tower, is all that remains of the convent founded by the Jesuits in the XVI century. The present church was built between the years 1681 and 1732, according to the plans drawn up by Josep Juli, from Barcelona, to replace the original, which burned down one hundred years earlier. The Salomonic columns flanking the statues of San Ignacio de Loyola and San Francisco de Borja, along with the profusion of volutes, are straight out of the Barroque. The interior decoration, also Barroque, was destroyed by a fire too, at the beginning of the Spanish Civil war in 1936. At that time, a large number of ecclesiastic buildings were destroyed in Barcelona.

The **Palau Moja** (I, D1) is across the street from the Church of Betlam; it is a fine example of secular architecture that dates from the XVIII century, built in accordance with the norms of the purest Neoclassical style. Its façade was decorated at the beginning of the XIX century by Josep Flaugier. The corredor

A fantastic dragon guards this corner of the Pla de la Boqueria.

between porticos was opened in 1934 to facilitate pedestrian traffic. At that same time, its splendid garden was destroyed. It used to be just behind the palace, but was replaced by private dwellings.

Once past the Carrer del Carme you will see on your right the sumptuous **Palau de la Virreina** (I, D1), which was built for Manuel Amat, Viceroy of Peru. The palace took its name from Amat's wife, since he died unexpectedly in the year 1779, hardly a year after the construction work had finished. The architect of the project is unknown, but the construction was directed by Carles Grau (1717-1798), who was the author of the decorative sculpture too. One outstanding feature of its façade is the enormous cornice that sustains the balustrade crowned by pitchers. Inside, in the central patio there is a twinned staircase. On the ground floor of the building there is an information service, and a bookstore specialized in artistic events of the city. Upstairs interesting expositions are held. Also on your right as you go down La Rambla you will see the city's best-known market, the **Mercat de Sant Josep** (I, D1), also known as the Boqueria market. It occupies the central patio of an interesting older square (from 1840), with porticos, which has been completely subjugated by the ironwork of the market's roof. Together with the common produce, rare and exotic foods are sold, all displayed in imaginative ways. The slang that the attendants use in their

The front of a pastry shop on Carrer Petxina, near the Pla de la Boqueria, an example of the Modernist style in Barcelona.

The Mercat de la Boqueria is the most popular in the city.

attempts to attract potential clients is also rather picturesque. On the same side of the street as the market there are several shops that display in their windows showy Modernist decoration. These anonymous works constitute vivid testimony to the depth of the roots of this artistic movement's roots in Catalan society at the turn of the century. In the Pla de la Boqueria you can still see traces of the medieval street layout. In this little square four streets meet, and the shape of their intersection indicates that one of the gates in the city wall that flanked the length of La Rambla was here. The streets from inside the city ran to this gate, and from it several roads set out. In the square today you will observe how the decorative styles from very different periods exist side-by-side. There is a Neoclassic **fountain** (1824), a large Chinese cast iron **dragon** on the corner of the house of Bruno Quadros, of Neo-Egyptian style (1896), and a **mosaic** in the centre of the square, by the painter Joan Miró, from Barcelona.

One of the four ways that cross the square (from the right as you go down La Rambla) is the Carrer Hospital.

Turn onto this street, and leave the central pavement of La Rambla for a while. You will come back to this same spot after a short side trip.

At number 10 of the street Carrer Hospital there is an eye-catching **house** with a Neoclassic-style façade (1849), decorated with terra-cotta motifs, something which is very common in Barcelona, used as a substitute for engraved decoration.

On the left you see the Barroque church **Iglesia de Sant Agustí Nou** (I, D1), begun in 1728 as an overly ambitious project, which was reduced in size twenty years later. In spite of the reduction, it is still huge today. It is composed of three naves with a cupola in the centre, and there is still one wing left of the two cloisters that it had. The façade is not quite as old as the rest; it is from the second half of the XVIII century, although, as you can see, it was never finished.

Through a Plateresque door at number 56 on Carrer Hospital you enter the premises of the old **Hospital de Santa Creu★★** (I, D1), today the headquarters of several cultural institutions. In

1401 the four hospitals that were in medieval Barcelona were merged into this one. The Gothic-style building consists of three naves of two floors each flanking a large rectangular patio, divided into two areas: the new one, presided over by a Barroque crucifix; and the Gothic one, made up of three wings of the cloister built in 1417 by Guillem Abiell. The architectural genious Antoni Gaudí died in a room of the hospital on June 7, 1926. At the end of the patio there is a portico, the entrance to the **Casa de Convalecencia,** where today you find the library **Biblioteca de Catalunya.** A Barroque construction from the xvii century, its building was directed by Andrés Bosch at first, then later by Josep Juli. In the vestibule there is a notable mural of polychromed ceramic tile (1684) that depicts various episodes from the life of San Pablo. A sculpture of the saint by Lluís Bonias (1677) presides over the patio. Through the library you can reach the Gothic naves of the Hospital, where reading rooms have been set up. Be sure not to miss the splendid **coffered ceiling** there.

Sculpture which depicts San Pablo, the work of L. Bonifàs, in the centre of the Baroque cloister of the Biblioteca de Catalunya.

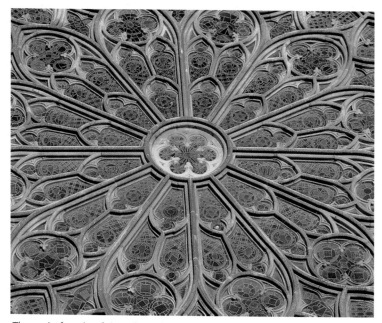

The main façade of the Iglesia del Pi is presided over by a huge rose window, a work from the Gothic period, although it was restored in this century.

Across the street from the Casa de Convelecencia you find the old surgeons' school, the **Colegio de Cirugía,** the seat of the Reial Academia de Medicina, in a Neoclassic building that follows the architectural norms of the period of Carlos III. The author of the project was the distinguished XVIII century surgeon Pere Virgili, whose bust presides over the curiously circular main hall.

The narrow street between the two buildings will take you to Carrer del Carme, which you should take back towards La Rambla again. At number 31 of Carrer del Carme there is a Neoclassic **house** whose façade is decorated by the technique of engraving multi-coloured layers of plaster.

Once you are back on La Rambla, you can cross over the prom-enade and take the street Carrer Portaferrissa, whose name comes from another gate in the medieval walls, decorated in iron or bronze. On the right you turn into the street Carrer Petritxol, a narrow little street, but very lively. Many people in Barcelona like to have an afternoon snack in one of its invitingly agreeable choco-late shops, especially when they are on a shopping trip, since there are many shops there too. The street goes to the Plaça del Pi, where you will see the **Iglesia del Pi**★ (I, D1). Although it was consecrated in 1453, its con-struction had begun a century and a half earlier. One of its mas-ter-builders was certainly Guillem Abiell. The church has a single nave with seven side chapels. But its most outstanding feature is the huge **rose window** in its main façade. The present stained glass is a faithful reproduction of what was destroyed by fire in 1936. Beside the lateral façade is a second square dedicated to San Josep Oriol, whose mortal remains rest in the church. An open-air market for the sale of paintings is set up periodically around the statue of the playwright Àngel Guimerà (1847-1924). On the wall of the church there is an inscription which commemorates a (possibly) miraculous event. Perhaps you will find it mildly amusing to read it. It goes like this: "On April 6, 1806 the news of the approval of the miracles of God's servant, Dr. José Oriol were spread, for which reason the exterior of the church was illuminated, and the director José Mestres, who was passing by at that moment, fell down like a brickstone to the ground from this little bridge, but got out unscathed, even though he was tramendously fat".

By going along the Carrer de Cecs you come to the Carrer de Boquería. Following it to the right, you come back to La Rambla again.

Going down La Rambla again, at a short distance on your right you will see the **Gran Teatre del Liceu★** (I, D1), inaugurated in 1848. The project was initially

The inside of the Gran Teatre del Liceu, a luxurious setting for the performance of the most select of opera works put on in Barcelona.

Petritxol

Catalonia has a reputation for being a place of deep-rooted traditions, carefully preserved by its people. The street Calle Petritxol might be considered the quintessence of this love of the traditional.

It is located in the neighbourhood of El Pi, beside La Rambla, and even though it is short and narrow, its shopkeepers and residents take good care of this colourful, lively street.

It seems that its name comes from a stone pilar that used to keep wagons from entering it. It is adorned with ceramic tiles bearing the names of people who used to live on it, people such as the playwright Angel Guimera; the colourful writer Pius Gener; and the scientist Sala i Campillo. But there is no memorial to Moratín, from Madrid, who lived on this street in 1814, when Petritxol was a squalid little street, as Moratín wrote then.

Typical attractions on this funny little street, among its many small places of business, are the two shops which sell hot chocolate with melindros and an old sweet shop, as well as the century-old Sala Parés, one of the most important art galeries in Barcelona; and the Librería Quera, a typical Catalan book shop, whose specialty is hiking and books related with the outdoors.

---

the work of Miquel Garriga, although it was rebuilt in the year 1862 after a devastating fire, by Josep Oriol Mestres. Its façade gives very little hint of the extraordinary size and sumptuousness of the inside of the theatre, both in the auditorium and the rest areas. Its layout has the shape of a horse-shoe, and it has 3,500 seats distributed between its ground floor and the five balconies. A majestic spiral staircase connects the vestibule with the first floor and the second.

The wealth of ornamentation decreases as you climb upwards, until when you reach the last gallery it is so dark you can hardly see. Besides, to get there you have to use another entrance door, the one on a side street. This stratification was supposed to reflect the prestige and position of the city's different social classes. It is not hard to understand, therefore, that in times of civil unrest the Liceu has been the scene of these struggles, too. For example, bombs were thrown from the upper gallery in 1893. A very peculiar group of people gather at the doors of the Liceu on the nights of the opera. It has become a veritable institution in Barcelona, and people attend as if they were fulfilling some ritual obligation.

The second cross-street on your left will take you directly to the **Plaça Reial** (I, D2). Laid out in the xix century not perfectly symmetrically, the uniformity of its façades attempts to compensate. Very interesting indeed are the Pasaje de Madoz and Pasaje de Bacardí that connect it to adjacent streets. Also interesting are the remains of the planning that Antoni Gaudí did for the square, and the three-armed fountain and street light that he designed. A few metres from la Rambla you can see one of Gaudí's first works, the **Palau Güell** (I, E2), located at number 3 of Carrer de Nou de la Rambla, almost in front of the Pasaje that goes to the Plaça Reial. The architectural genius designed this palace to be the residence of the industrialist and maecenas Eusebi Güell, whose name is now linked forever with that of Gaudí. The latter provided the artistic imagination, while the former provided the sensitivity and conviction that allowed Gaudí to put his ideas into stone and iron.

Water and palm trees create a pleasant atmosphere of this square.

The construction of the Palau Güell coincided with the period of the urban boom brought about by the Exposicón Universal in 1888. Dotted with Neogothic features, the façade is grandly sober. The high point of the house's architecture is the treatment of volumes in it, and the ornamentation of its interior. Some of the rooms are open to visitors since the building houses

One can pause to rest or watch the flow of people from one of the many sidewalk cafés on the Plaça Reial.

Pleasure craft in Barcelona's harbour.

the **Museo del Arte Escénico** (I, E2).

At number 8 of La Rambla you can see the Neoclassic **Palau Marc** (I, E2), from 1776, and across from it you find what once was an old Augustine convent, later to be made into the parish **Church of Santa Mònica** (I, E2), to which has been added .the **Centro de Arte Contemporáneo.**

❖ Portal de la Pau (I, E2)

In the same period of time when a gate was opened in the wall to facilitate access to what is today the Plaça de Catalunya, another opening was made in this part of the wall in 1849 to facilitate access to the port. This new gate was called Portal de la Pau. The **Monument to Colón★** (I, E2) (Christopher Columbus) presides over the square, on top of a spectacular iron column some 50 metres high, put up in 1886. A lift will take you up to the viewpoint at the foot of this huge statue, where you will get a splendid view of the city and the harbour. If you were to follow along in the direction that the statue seems to indicate with outstretched arm, symbolically pointing to the lands of America, you would never reach this continent; or only after having gone around the globe. In any case, you were warned in the beginning that directions in Barcelona are far from standard, and do not conform to the usual points of the compass.

But the most interesting feature of this area, and one of the most notable of the city, is the architectural group of the **Reials Drassanes★★** (I, F2), an exceptional case of the preservation of a medieval shipyard. Its masterbuilder was Arnau Ferrer. The first eight parallel naves were finished in 1381, but in 1390 they planned to enlarge the structure to provide space for as many as 30 ships. At the beginning of the XVII century they built the three eastern naves, and from 1663 on the shipyard became a military barracks and arsenal. At that time they built the bulwark that defended it. From the oldest part, the part built under King Pere "el Gran", there are two crenallated towers left in the western side. Of the eight naves built by King Pere "el Ceremoniós", seven remain today (plus three of a later date of construction) as a result of the joining of the two central ones in the XVIII century.

The work on the commercial premises of the harbour **puerto de Barcelona** was also begun in the Portal de la Pau. You can visit them by making a pleasant boat trip to the breakwater in the popular "golondrinas", tourist boats that dock at a neighbouring pier. Once on the breakwater, you can take a stroll along the length of the structure, or have a drink in one of the terraces facing the Mediterranean, before catching the next boat back to land.

❖ Passeig Colom (I, E2)

The Passeig Colom goes all along the full length of what once was the medieval wall, torn down in 1881. After its inauguration, it became one of the busiest routes in the city.

To a certain extent it took over the function of Carrer Ample (which goes along parallel but inside the walled area) when it connected the Drassanes with the Llotja, the two economically important centres of activity in the city. Today this same journey can be made past the restored **Moll de la Fusta** (I, E3), whose name commemorates the lumber yard that was for decades a veritable barrier separating the city from the sea. The new Moll de la Fusta, built up in the last part of the eighties, is also a symbol of the maritime role of Barcelona, the fruit of municipal initiative that continues on other piers, previously dedicated to the

From the viewpoint of the Monument to Columbus, in El Portal de la Pau, you can get a magnificent view of Barcelona's harbour.

El Consolat de Mar

One of the most important Catalan institutions in the Middle Ages was the Consolat de Mar, a tribunal with jurisdiction over the business affairs of the merchant navy. The oldest surviving written ref-

erence to it is from the Barcelona of 1282, prior to those which refer to Majorca and Valencia, kingdoms that were governed by the maritime customs of Barcelona. The first Consulate must have been set up in the city around 1250. Its laws were gathered together in the famous book Llibre del Consolat de Mar, *from the middle of the XIV century. The oldest copy of this book of orders, customs and maritime and commercial regulations is in Majorca, while Barcelona has a copy in the Biblioteca de Catalunya. The Tribunal met in Barcelona, and was presided over by two Counselors, advised by merchants and jurists. There were Consulate offices which represented the Tribunal in the almost all of the ports on the shore of the Mediterranean Sea, in both Europe and Africa. The old and very appealing street Calle del Consolat de Mar runs into the Plaza de Palacio and alongside the Gothic Lonja, which is inside the building of the Cámara de Industria, Comercio y Navegación.*

commercial activities of the port and today open to all citizens. The Moll de la Fusta has two storeys connected by movable bridges. On the lower level the old stone paving of the pier has been retained, and in fact pleasure craft and ships related in some way to the city's image promotion still tie up there. The upper storey was planned to be a balcony looking out onto the Mediterranean Sea. Bars and restaurants have taken charge of charging up the atmosphere there. A most oriental kiosk there, crowned by a giant prawn, was designed by Mariscal (who also designed the Barcelona mascot-logo for the 1992 Olympic Games). The group of Moll de la Fusta is the work of the architect Manuel de Sola Morales.

Once again on the Passeig Colom, the building that has number 2 above its door is known locally as the **Casa de Cervantes** (I, D-E3), due to the belief that the author of *El Quijote* resided in it on his visits to the city. It is true that Cervantes did culminate his adventures as an errant knight in Barcelona. The house was completely reformed in the XX century, although it has preserved some of its original features from the XVI century. The adjoining building displays some Rococo plasterwork engravings from the XVIII century on its façade.

❖ Passeig d'Isabel II and Pla del Palau (I, D3)

The extension of Passeig de Colom is named Passeig d'Isabel II, and occupies the terrain of the old wall too. The wall was torn

From the Monument to Columbus in El Portal de la Pau there is a magnificent view of the harbour.

down to make room for rows of trees, which have since sadly disappeared. On the slope of the mountain is the **Llotja★** (I, D3), the commodity exchange in Barcelona since the Middle Ages, and emblem of the commercial apogee of the city. The original building was put up right on the sea-shore during the second half of the XIV century. Its splendidly high-cielinged Gothic hall, concluded in 1329 by Pere Arvey, along with some arches more than 10 m high are all that are left of it. This hall is today the home of the trading sessions of the Barcelona Stock Exchange. In the XVIII century the original nave was completely reformed and made into the present Neoclassic one. It was inaugurated in the year 1802, as a jewel of the architecture of that time.

On the side of the sea there is a building with portico, the **Casa de Xifré** (I, D3), from 1840. Besides its Neoclassic façade, it has outstanding terra-cotta medallions with allegoric themes decorating the arches of the porch, all typical of the architecture of Barcelona. On the ground floor is the **Café de las Siete Puertas** (I, D3), today made into a restaurant only. It was set up in business by José Cuyas, a famous café proprietor who never would reveal the enigma of the name he gave to the café, as it has eight doors, (not "siete"). The opening of this café marked a milestone in the quotidian attitudes of the cityfolk, as it managed to bring about a change in the reputation of the institution of the "café", which had always

been considered before to be a disreputable place. This block of dwellings was also the first home of the family of Picasso, on their arrival in the city in 1895.

The Passeig d'Isabel II runs into the Plaça del Pla del Palau, built up in 1825 with monumental ambitions, and the intention of making it the new heart of the city. Its white marble central fountain, by Francesc Daniel i Molina, is dedicated to the "Catalan Genius". On the other side of the square was the Palau Reial, which gave its name to the Plaça before it was destroyed by fire in 1875. Across from it is the old customs building, seat of the **Gobierno Civil** (I, C-D3), since 1902, a Neoclassic building from the last decade of the XVII century. To get to the Basilica de Santa María del Mar you leave the square by a narrow street that begins on the side of the mountain, called Carrer de Espaseria. Its name commemorates the organization of the medieval Barcelona guild which was responsible for manufacturing swords and other arms, a flourishing business which earned a high reputation for quality products throughout the Mediterranean basin.

❖ Santa Maria del Mar★★ (I, C3)

In front of the church Iglesia de Santa Maria del Mar is the square of the same name, a typical enclave which was originally a cemetery. It sits on top of land which was freed by the outlawing of parish cemeteries. In the square there is a Gothic **foun-**

tain from 1402 with three spouts. Behind it is the street Carrer Caputxes, followed by Carrer de Canvis Vells. Both of them still retain there magnificent medieval aspect.

On the spot where the church stands today, there must have been a previous one in which Santa Eulalia was buried, according to legend. Devotion to this saint has always been particularly fervent in the city. The work on the Basilica was begun in 1329. Fifty years later it was completly finished, a very exceptional case of this type of cathedral constructions, which usually took a century or two. It was probably the result of the economic bonanza that befell the city after its Mediterranean conquests, which followed one after the other. The work seems to have been directed by Berenguer de Montagut. It is composed of a central, very

An elegant staircase with balustrade form the Llotja, a sober composition, emblematic of Barcelona's commercial apogee.

Overwhelming, stylized interior of Santa Maria del Mar, one of the most extraordinarly pure Gothic works in Barcelona.

wide nave and two narrower side ones. The three are of roughly equal height. Disasters throughout history have considerably shrunk the reserves of interior

A thirsting Christ showing his stigmata in Santa Maria del Mar.

decoration housed in its chapels and altars. Two octagonal towers flank the main façade, on whose door are the images of San Pedro and San Pablo. The rose window that crowns the building dates from the xv century and replaced the original one, lost in an earthquake.

Across the Carrer Sant Maria, on one side, is the Fosser de les Moreres, a minor cemetery of the church where those who died in the defense of Barcelona during the siege of 1714 were buried. If you go around the church on the outside, at the level of the apse is another door which was built in the xvi century. This one opens onto the Passeig de Born, in an area where in the old days they held jousts, tournaments and military celebrations. It is thus one of the corners of the city with the greatest number of historical associations. At the end of the Passeig is the old market **mercat de Abasts del Born** (I, C3), a splendid example of cast-iron architecture from the second half of the XIX century. Today its large open area is used for cultural events. Around it experimental and vanguard art galleries have been established; the one called **Metronom,** set up in the warehouse at Carrer Fusina, 9, is especially interesting.

❖ Carrer Montcada★★ (I, C3)

The little square of Montcada is located beside the door in the apse of Santa María del Mar, where Carrer Montcada enters the Passeig del Born. It surely is one of the most notable in the city, due to its history and monumentality.

The entire length of the Carrer Montcada could be considered to be a museum of secular architecture in Barcelona, with fine examples from each of its many centuries of existence.

The success of this street is due to the fact that it linked the commercial area with the seafront, first of all, and secondly, it was on the way to the Basilica of Santa María del Mar, after the church was built. The date of the street's origin is ususally given as the year 1148, in the times of Ramon Berenguer IV. At that time a group of merchants from Barcelona, led by Guillem Ramon de Montcada, obtained permission to build in the area, which was nothing more than a deserted, sandy place crossed by a small dry wash. The permission was granted as a reward for their having participated in the con-

quest of Tortosa. The period of the street's greatest splendour lasted from the XIV to the XVII century. It was then lined with splendid palaces and dwellings that were, in many cases, used as residences of honour by distinguished visitors.

In the case of the houses most typical of the street, a semicircular arch built of voussoirs forms the entrance to a spacious, open patio, from which a stairway climbs to the main entrance of the house. The façade is completed by a veranda and a low tower from where the beach can be seen, along with the merchant ships that might be approaching the city. This is the most common Gothic model.

With the opening up of over-

El Passeig del Born, situated in the very heart of the Barrio Gótico.

seas commerce to the Catalans in the XVIII century, the financial and commercial centre of the city moved to Carrer Ample, nearer the port, which was to mean the decline of Carrer Montacada. During the XIX century the decline accelerated sharply, but then after the decade of the thirties in this century the townsfolk demanded that the authorities do something to restore and preserve the buildings of this street, the emblem of the patrimonial wealth of Barcelona.

At number 20 on Carrer Montcada you will see one of its most splendid palaces, the **Casa Dalmesas,** typical Baroque architecture which replaced a previously existing palace in the XVII century. Of the original a **chapel** from the XV century remains, along with some other architectural details. A lovely group of sculptured angels playing different musical instruments decorate the arches of the chapel.

The most distinguished resident of this house was Pau Ignasi de Dalmesas, who lived from 1670 to 1718, was the first chronicler of the city, and the founder of the distinguished Academia de los Desconfiados. At number 25 is the **Casa Cervelló** (I, C3) from the XV century, which shows off a magnificently preserved Renaissance façade with its outstanding ashlars. Today it houses a fine gallery of art.

The **house** at number 23 is the oldest on the street, from the XIV century, and still retains its tower, typical of the zone ("miramar"), from where a lookout could watch the sea for signs of the arrival of an interesting ship. The house also has a window in the shape of a triptych, the ancient symbol of aristocracy.

The **house** at number 18, from the XV-XVI centuries, has a unique enclosed arcade on the upper part of its façade, while the one at number 14 is a Gothic-Renaissance **palace** with posterior Neoclassic reforms.

The **Palau del Marqués de Lió** (I, C3), at number 12, maintains its original structure dating from the XIV century (with its tower and Gothic windows). Renaissance features (windows and doors), as well as Baroque (patio and staircase), were added in successive reforms. Across from this palace is the **Palau Aguilar,** since 1963 the seat of the **Museo Picasso** in Barcelona. It is a notable building from the XV century on which Marc Safont seems to have worked. He was also the author of the Gothic façade of the Palau de la Generalitat. The most outstanding feature of the building is doubtlessly its lovely open patio with the staircase and sculpted decorational motifs.

The building up of the Carrer de la Princesa divided Carrer Montcada into two sections.

Although on the other stretch there are no longer buildings of as great an interest as the preceding ones, it is still a good idea to go ahead on the street to visit the little square of the XII century Romanesque chapel **Capilla de Marcús** (I, C3). It is built at the foot of the road that from the time of the Romans crossed the

The quarter Barrio del Born is one of the residential neighbourhoods in Barcelona, where old professions are still pursued.

city lengthwise. In the area of the square of Marcús this street changes its name from Carders on the right, to Corders on the left. Like those of other streets, both names refer to skills related with the textile industry, and are testimony to the guild origins of the street.

If you turn to the left on Carrer Corders it will take you to the Plaça de la Llana, and further on, to where Carrer Boria joins the Via Laietana. This stretch of street will leave you with an impression that is completely different from that of the aristocratic Carrer Montcada, but none the less still typical of Barcelona. Its lively atmosphere and the hustle and bustle of the residents going about their quotidian activities are what make it so appealing.

❖ **Plaça Ramon Berenguer III and Plaça del Rei** (I, C2).

Once you reach the Via Laietana you should turn right towards the mountain, and within 25 m you will find on your left as you climb up the street the Plaça Ramon Berenguer III, with its bronze **statue** of the great king on horseback, the work of Josep Llimona (1864-1934).

This little square makes an ideal spot from which to see the part of the **wall**★★ that enclosed the Roman town in the time of the empire. It seems that the original fortifications of the colony, founded in the area of the low knoll, the *Mons Taber,* between the Besós and Llobregat Rivers, were not strong enough to withstand the attacks of the Visigoths, who completely destroyed

Façade of the Palau Cervelló, which is found on Carrer Montcada, one of the oldest and most monumental streets in Barcelona.

Picasso in Barcelona

Pablo Ruiz Picasso was born in Malaga in 1881, but spent his childhood and early youth in Barcelona, between 1895 and 1904. In spite of the fact that he spent the rest of his life in France, he always considered himself to be Spanish and even Catalan. He left a fine collection of his early work, and some from later periods, to the city of Barcelona. It is housed

in the museum that bears his name in the old street of Montcada. During his years in Barcelona Picasso lived the life of the city intensely, and made close friends here, friendships which lasted throughout his years in Paris.

He lived with his parents and sister in the Plaza de la Merced, and studied drawing and painting in the school of Bellas Artes de Llotja. Furthermore, he set up and used several painting studios, at Calle de la Platja, 4; Escudellers Blancs, 1 and 2; Nou de la Rambla, 10; and Comercio, 18.

He used to meet his friends in the tavern Els Quatre Gats, where he chatted with Santiago Rusiñol and Ramon Casas. He frequented such night spots as the Edén Concert on Nou de la Rambla. He put on an exposition in the Sala Parés, on Calle Petritxol, and his famous painting entitled Las Señoritas de Avignon *is suposed to have been inspired by the brothel on the Calle Avinyó.*

the colony in the third century, according to archaeological evidence. Afterwards the Romans decided to build the imposing wall of which, fortunately, a stretch still remains to be seen in this square, in places forming an integral part of the buildings erected later.

Judging from the length of the wall, which enclosed a rectangle of 1,270 m on its longest side, we should say that the Roman town was not very large, although it certainly was well defended by its robust walls. As you will be able to observe, towers almost ten metres high and six metres wide were spaced along the length of four-metre thick wall. Both the towers and walls were built of huge ashlars, perhaps taken from buildings destroyed in the siege of the original colony. In the nearby **Museu d'Historia de la Ciutat** you can see the interior structure of the wall, and also see that many of the ashlars still bear inscriptions carved for their former use.

During the Middle Ages arches were built between one tower and the next, so that the wall could be used in posterior constructions. This is the case of the wall you can see in the Plaça Ramon Berenguer III, since the **Capilla Reial de Santa Àgata** was built on top of a stretch of the Roman wall. This Gothic church from the XIV century forms a part of one of the city's most interest-

Interior view of the magnificent Gothic Chapel of Santa Àgata.

ing monumental groups, the **Palau Reial Maior**★★ (I, C2). To reach it, leave the square by taking Carrer Tapineria towards the sea, and once you reach the Plaça del Àngel turn right onto the street Bajada de Llibreteria. One of the four entrance gates to the fortified Roman town was in Plaça del Angel until the middle of the XIX century. The first street to the right leads to the Plaça del Rei, but before you get there you will pass the **Museu d'Historia de la Ciutat** (I, C2) in an enormous house on Carrer Veguer. This typically Catalan Gothic house (XV-XVI centuries) was moved here from its original site on the neighbouring Carrer Mercaders.

As you enter the Plaça del Rei, the monumental building you will see to your right is the chapel **Capilla Reial de Santa Àgata** (I, C2), whose walls, resting on the roman fortification, can be seen from the Plaça Ramon Berenguer III. Immediately across the square is the palace Palau Reial Major, which was the residence of the Counts of Barcelona from the IX century. It is highly possible that it was the residence of the Visigoth kings too, in previous centuries. Ataúlfo had set up his Court in the city in the V century. Perhaps even the Roman Praetors stayed in it. There are three large arches in its **façade** that join the bulwarks of the building, and are adjoined to the walls of the original Romanesque palace (XII century), ordered built by Ramon Berenguer IV.

The Romanesque windows of

In the Plaça del Rei is the Palau Reial Maior, which was the residence of the Counts of Barcelona from the IX century.

the palace were bricked over on the outside, although you can still see them from the inside. To replace them, some triptych windows were built first, and then later the Gothic rose windows. A semicircular staircase leads up to the entrance to the **Capilla Reial** (I, C2) and the palace of the Count, of which there is still a magnificent ambassador's hall left, called the **Saló del Tinell,** built by King Pere "el Ceremoniós" in the XIV century. It is a large rectangular hall whose cieling rests on six semicircular stone arches with embedded pillars. Master Guillem Carbonell direct-

ed the project. It was the monarchs' favourite spot for the celebration of the most solemn of events.

On the left in the square you find the palace **Palau del Lloctinent ★** (I, C2), headquarters for the archives of the Crown of Aragón, a Renaissance palace from the XVI century built according to plans drawn up by Antoni Carbonell. From the same period is the embedded **watch tower,** called "el Mirador", of King Martí, which occupies a corner of the square. A piece of sculpture by Chillida was recently placed in the square.

You can take the street Bajada de Santa Clara out of the square, going along outside the Palau del Lloctinent, in which is the entrance gate to the Carrer Comtes. At this corner you turn left onto the Carrer Freneria, and then turn right onto Carrer Llibreteria, which leads directly to the Plaça de Sant Jaume. On this street there are some extremely personalized shops, such as the Cereria Subirana, which retains its marvellous eighteenth century decoration.

❖ Plaça de Sant Jaume★ (I, D2)

For many centuries the Plaça de Sant Jaume was the centre of the fortified city, at the intersection of the Roman roads that crossed vertically and horizontally. This

Gothic-style "twinned" window of the Palau Real.

intersection has witnessed many of the important events in the history of Barcelona, and the grandeur of the buildings that flank it is a reflection of the degree of authority invested in the city's institutions. The municipal government has been housed here since the XIV century, on the lower side, and the autonomous government occupies the other side; the two buildings have been face to face since the final construction on the square in 1823.

In the year 1373 the council that governed the city, the Consell de Cent, inaugurated a hall to hold its meetings, called the **Saló de Cent** (still in existence today). Since that time the building **Casa de la Ciutat★★** (I, D2) (at present Barcelona's city Hall) has been subject to several enlargements and reforms on a considerable scale. The last of them, carried out during the decades of the thirties and forties in the XIX century, endowed the Gothic building with a monumental **façade.** Although its features are uniformly Neoclassic, you can percieve a certain antagonism between two different conceptions within one and the same style. As a whole, the work is characterized by Helenic ideas of austerity and purity, defended by the architect Josep Mas i Vila, the author of the project. But once the project was completed, the architect Fransesc Daniel i Molina, who was more fond of an academic Neoclassic style, designed the group of sculptures that crown the façade. The statues of

Jaume I and the counsellor Joan Fiveller, the work of the sculptor Josep Bover Mas, decorate the main entrance.

Of much more historic interest is the Gothic **façade** that gives onto the Carrer Ciutat, built at the end of the XIV century under the direction of Arnau Bagués. The predominantly horizontal lines of the façade are presided over by the interesting statue of the Archangel San Rafael, by an anonymous sculptor, to which later were affixed two bronze wings. The rest of the sculptures is also of a notable quality.

In the interior of the Casa de la Ciutat you can see, besides the previously-mentioned Saló de Cent, the Gothic **patio** and **arcade,** as well as the **Saló de Croniques** (1929), decorated with some impressive mural paintings by Josep María Sert.

On the other side of the square is the **Palau de la Generalitat de Catalunya★★** (I, D2), headquarters of the autonomous government.

The origins of this institution have been fixed in the XII century, during the reigns of Jaume I and Perer "el Ceremoniós". Since then it has governed the destiny of the Catalan people, until its abolition in the XVIII century by Felipe V, who favoured central government. It was restored to power briefly, during the Republican period (1931-1939), and again in the year 1979. However, the building that houses it is from the XV century. The original main façade, that opens onto Carrer Sant Honorat, was the

One can see the sculpture of San Jordi slaying the dragon , the work of Andreu Aleu, in the Renaissance façade of the Palau de la Generalitat.

Arcade of the Palau de la Generalitat, a work whose beautiful, graceful elegance is due to the fineness of the columns that support its arches.

work of Marc Safont, who also was the author of its **patio,** its Gothic **staircase** and the lovely **Capilla de Sant Jordi,** which is safe inside. The Renaissance **façade** that gives onto the Plaça de Sant Jaume was built at the end of the xvi century by Pere Blay, incorporating very Italianized features. Above the main balcony is the outstanding statue of Sant Jordi sculpted by Andreu Aleu in 1867. On the façade of Carrer del Bisbe there is on the left a Gothic door from the xv century presided over by a splendid medallion of Sant Jordi sculpted by Pere Joan.

Passing over the Neogothic bridge (perhaps a bit macabre in its inspiration, from 1928), you find, at the corner of Carrer Pietat, the door from an enlargement project from the xvi century.

In a little square at the end of the street is an exposition of a group of sculptures by Josep Llimona. The Carrer del Bisbe leads you from the Plaça de Sant Jaume, with its civil government headquarters, to the area of the Cathedral, the spiritual heart of the city.

❖ The Cathedral★★ (I, C2)

There are documents that indicate that a very large Visigoth church, and another Romanesque one (xi century), existed on the present site of the Gothic Basilica, the Cathedral of Barcelona.

In May of 1298 work was begun on the Cathedral, which was not to be finished until this xx century. Even though the basic structure could be considered to have been finished in 1448, the main façade and its two ornamental towers were built between 1887 and 1913.

If you go around the outside of the Cathedral in a clockwise direction, your eye will be caught firstly, in Carrer Comtes, by a sculpted boot in a stone at the height of the second lower window. The group of five upper windows is made up of two Flamboyant-style, and three of a style closer to the original of the Basilica, from the XIV century.

At the end of the wall, in the oldest part of the church, is the door **Puerta de Sant Iu,** splendidly severe and balanced. Going around the apse, on Carrer Pietat, you come across the two doors from the XV century that open directly onto the cloister. The other door, the Puerta de Santa Eulalia, is on Carrer del Bisbe.

On the corner of the street is the chapel **Capilla de Santa Llúcia,** a transition Romanesque church built thirty years before the beginning of the Basilica, and incorporated later within the Cathedral.

Once inside, the most striking feature in the central nave, one of three, are the imposing **choirstalls.** Bishop Ramon d'Escales had them built in the year 1380.

The most famous sculptors of that time worked on their carvings. Jordi Johan was the first, and then in the xv century came Anglada and Macia Bonafé, who finished the job in 1459.

In the XVI century, the fine sculptor Bartolomé Ordóñez carved the screens that decorate the entrances to the choir; he was not able to finish those of the retrochoir.

In front of the main altar there is a staircase that leads down into the **crypt,** presided over by the sepulchre of Santa Eulalia, from the XIV century. In the direction of the main entrance you find the old Sala Capitular, made into the **Capilla del Cristo de Lepanto** (also called Chapel of Sant Oleguer). In it there is both the carved crucifix (XVI century) that Juan de Austria took with him into the battle of Lepanto, and the recumbent statue of the saint, the work of Pere Sanglada(1490). But the place that is without a doubt the most inviting in the Cathedral is its **cloister,** thanks above all to its sublime garden with its tall palm trees and rotund magno-

Everything is lovely in the cloister of the Cathedral of Barcelona.

A view of the imposing monumental group formed by the Chapel of Santa Àgata, the Palau del Lloctinent, and Barcelona's Cathedral.

lias growing round a pool where the quacking ducks have set up their kingdom.

In a corner a murmuring fountain grants the wishes of visitors if they throw coins into it. In one of its chapels you can see a group of sculptures by Llimona, and above one of the arches there is a statue of Sant Jordi from the XVI century, the work of Antoni Claperós.

In the area of the Cathedral there are some buildings that are directly related with it. Across from the Chapel of Santa Llúcia a tall palm sticks up above the façade of the **Casa del Ardiaca** (I, C2), which houses the Archivo Hitórico of the city, in a late Gothic (XV century) building whose U-shaped floor plan encloses the patio where the palm tree grows.

Still on the Carrer del Bisbe you can see the **Palau Episcopal** (I, C2). Only the patio is left from its original, XII century construction. The present façade was done in the XVIII century. On the other side of the Cathedral, flanking the staircase which goes from the Basilica to the Avenue, you find the building of the **Canonja i Pia Almoina** (I, C2), whose two parts are built of stone, one from the XV, and the other from the XVI century.

❖ Plaça Nova★★ (I, C2)

Contrary to what its name might seem to indicate (New Square), Plaça Nova is not new; there is documental evidence that it has existed at the gate of the Roman walls since the XV century.

In that time its role in the medieval city was two-fold. First-ly, from it roads went off through the flatlands of Barcelona in the direction of the village of Gracia; and secondly, and more importantly, it became the site of an open-air commodities market that later became the place for buying and selling furniture and other objects of domestic use. As a legacy of its past, a natural alinement links it directly to the Passeig de Gracia; and there are antique shops on some of its neighbouring streets; and the names of those same streets.

But the most characteristic features of the present-day Plaça Nova are its well-maintained semicircular **towers** that once flanked the gates of the fortified Roman settlement (the towers that flanked the other three gates were torn down in the past century). A part of the neighbouring buildings were built on top of the imposing Roman ashlars (the case of the Casa del Ardiaca and the Palau Episcopal).

In the tower on the left there is a **niche** with a statue of Sant Roc, the saint the people of Barcelona invoked with particular devotion so that he might protect them from the much-feared plague.

During centuries the square had a different look that was completed by the Roman arch that joined the towers, and the aqueduct that was borne on them. In the beginnings of the XVII century they built an arcade with portico to house the water reservoirs. All of that disappeared in 1823 to make way for the Carrer del Bisbe.

(At this point you can start the special itinerary through the Gothic quarter, Barrio Gótico, which is detailed after this section.)

On the other side of the square is the eight-storey **Edifice of the Colegio de Arquitectos** (I, C1-2) (1962), a complete mismatch for the group of Gothic buildings around it. Outstanding modern engravings in plaster, designed by Picasso, decorate its façade. Inside it, two more mural paintings by the genius of a painter from Malaga are on display.

You should leave the square on the Carrer de Arcs, a street named after the Roman aqueduct that came through here to supply the city's water.

Next comes the Portal d'Arcs, a crowded pedestrian zone where a lot of shops have been set up to sell fashionable clothing. At number 22 of the street, the **Compañía del Gas** (I, C1)has set up its offices in a Modernist building (1895), not really a very

---

Colonia Iulia, Augusta, Faventia, Paterna Barcino

In the year 13 or 15 BC, that is to say, a little more than two thousand years ago, the Romans set up a colony and gave it the above (perhaps overly long) name. Over the years, the name was reduced to Barcelona. It was a half-military, half-commercial colony, much smaller than that of Tarraco, the capital of the region and had its moment of greatest splendour in the II century (with aqueducts and thermal baths); in the year 300 it was still a strategically important enclave, as bear witness its high, robust walls. Thanks to these walls, Barcelona was able to become the melting pot of Catalonia in the Middle Ages.

Barcino was built on a low hill called "el Taber". On its highest point (12 m above sea level) the Cathedral was built centuries later. As were most Roman colonies, it was rectangular shaped within its walls and had two main streets, Cardo and Decumanus, which intersected at the forum (an elongate square). The forum was the colony's political, military, religious social and commercial centre.

The population within the walls of Barcina was not very large, as there were only 50 or so stately homes, with their storage space for wheat and wine presses and cellars. Actually, the town was active in business, as were all the rest of the communities in the area that is today known as Barcelona. Divided up into farming estates, each of them had their workshops for the production of consumer goods that were sent on, in large part, to the Roman troops who faced the Visigoths in the area of the Rhine. The position of Barcelona's harbour, close to the centres of production and sheltered by the slopes of Montjuïc, off to the east made the city strategically important. All of this history becomes even more interesting when you visit the archaeological digs in under the Plaça del Rei (in the Museo de Historia de la Ciudad), where you find the remains of Barcino on the same spot where it once flourished.

creative work, and with a defi-
nite tendency to take itself too
seriously.

You can continue along the
pedestrian area by turning to the
right, once you pass the last
building, along the Carrer Com-
tal until you reach the Via Laietana.

❖ Palau de la Música Catalana (I, B-C2)

At the intersection of Via Laietana with Sant Pere Més Alt the
guild of the Arte Mayor de la
Seda (silk) had its headquarters.
There it had the **Casa dels Vel-
ers** (I, C2) built in 1763. The
building's magnificent Barroque-
style engravings in plaster decorate two of its three façades. The
one that looks onto the Plaça
Lluís Millet displays an unfortunate reproduction of the original
drawings.

*Modernism sought for the synthesis
of music, sculpture and painting.*

On the other side of this little
square you can see one of the
most representative examples of
the fertile Modernism movement
in Barcelona, the **Palau de la
Música Catalana★★,** the work
of the architect Lluís Domènech
i Montaner. He designed it in
1908 to be a concert hall for the
Orfeó Catala, although its much
more ambitious symbolic meaning pointed towards the rebirth
of Catalan art. The rising industrial barons were to sponsor this
rebirth, through their need for
external signs of cultural and
political identity.

As is normally the case in Modernist buildings, both on the outside and inside, the decorative
arts (ceramic tile coverings,
stained glass windows, mosaics,
reliefs...), the groups of sculptures by Miquel Blay and Eusebi
Arnau, and the architectural
structures merge to form a
unique ambient, full of symbolic
features and imaginative opulence.

In the concert hall there are
sculptures on both sides of the
stage. Those on the left are
presided over by a bust of Clavé,
while over those on the right is
a bust of Beethoven. The vegetal
motifs that frame the former
was the work of Pay Gargallo.
Both on the outside of this grand
concert hall and inside it, there is
not a single corner which is not
loaded with graceful ornamen-

Palau de la Música, the Modernist work of Domènech i Montaner, which combines spectacular sculpture, painting and architecture.

tation. A group of architects directed by Óscar Tusquets thoroughly reformed the Palau in the late eighties, while carefully respecting its original spirit.

Once again on the Via Laietana, this time going up it, the Neoclassic building that houses the offices of **La Caixa** (I, B1) will catch your eye. It was a work from late in the career of Enric Sagnier, from year 1917.

It would be a good idea to walk on the left side of the street, and keep your eye on the ground —something not ususally recommended to visitors—, because in front of building number 69 there is an unususal illuminated clock at ground level on the pavement. It was built in 1935 and restored in 1989.

Your journey on this itinerary concludes in the Plaça Urquinaona, a few steps from where it began.

After having seen all the vestiges of the past on the streets and avenues of the city, here you have a square that gave in to modern times and their most visible symbol: the skyscraper. There are two skyscrapers on this square, although the passing of the years has demoted their category, in terms of their ranking according to height. The one of only fifteen storeys is on the corner of Carrer Jonqueres and Trafalgar, a functional job from the decade of the forties, although it was designed before the Civil War. On the corner of Carrer Roger de Llúria is the other higher one, built at the end of the decade of the sixties. ◆

Barrio Gótico (The Gothic Quarter)

In the place where the old part of Barcelona is located, on a low elevation that the Romans called *Mons Taber,* the inhabitants of the original colony of *Barcino* erected a temple dedicated to the Emperor Augustus in the first century AD. In addition to the archaeologic remains from that period, there are others from the earlier Iberic tribes who inhabited these lands. But the events that conditioned the city and largely made it what it is today began in the third century AD, when the Roman wall was built. The economic and military dominance of Barcelona in the centuries that followed was doubtlessly due to those robust Roman walls. The conquest of the Mediterranean basin was launched from those walls by the Counts and Kings of the Crown of Aragón, after the Visigoths had made some initial attempts at such expansion.

The direct result of their domination is the monumental Barrio Gótico. People started referring to it as the "Gothic Quarter" around the date of 1926, due to its having been built during the Ogival period, between the XIII and XV centuries, the city's time of greatest splendour. That is why the Gothic the most associated is style with old Barcelona. Curiously, it is also associated with modern Barcelona, since the architectural style most used by the flourishing Modernists was the Neogothic. Perhaps the architects were hoping to recapture some of the splendours of the past.

The route that you will find described herein is designed to be a supplementary tour, which pays attention above all to the old architecture of the city's streets and squares, and the beauty of the many quiet corners which outshines their anonymity.

This itinerary begins in the Plaça Nova, at the gates of the Roman stronghold, and continues along to the left on Carrer de la Palla. The streets name comes from the weight of the straw that used to be stored on it. And if the street name is a direct legacy of the medieval market held here, so also are the many

The inside of an antique shop in the Barrio Gótico.

antique shops that keep on doing business in the area.

The curving layout of this street is a clear reflection of the fact that it once ran along outside the curving city wall. In fact, you can still see a perfectly preserved fragment of two **towers** with a stretch of city wall in a little square of modern design on the left. Further ahead, where this street forks, the curving way continues along Carrer Banys Nous. At number 20 on this street there is a typical Barcelona-style tavern, El Portalón, whose lugubrious looks have not deterred many groups of artists from meeting there. Perhaps they are feeling nostalgic about the secret meetings of anarchist-workers in the beginning of this century.

Turn to the left on the first street that you cross, the Bajada de Santa Eulalia, to reach the inside of what was the Roman town. The steepness of the street and its name ("bajada") are a reflection of the fact that when the wall's military usefulness came to an end in the XIII century, openings were made in it. The difference in elevation between the interior and exterior was accounted for by "bajadas" (stairs), common in all the old walled perimeter.

The first street to the left leads to the **Plaça Sant Felip Neri★** (I, D2), which is generally a very quiet corner, except for the time of day when it is invaded by children from the school set up in the old **Casa del Gremi de Calderers** (I, D2). The children are released from the XVI century Renaissance building moved here from its orig-

inal site on the Carrer Boria to make room for the construction of the Via Laietana. The other Renaissance **house** on the square, today the seat of the **Museo del Calzado Antiguo** (I, D2) (1565), was also built on another street (that no longer exists) and moved in 1943 to its present site. The only monumental building that was constructed on the square is the **church,** which dates from the middle of the XVIII century.

After leaving the square of Sant Felip Neri, at number 9 on Carrer Sant Sever you will see a **church** (I, D2) from the beginnings of the XVIII century with interesting Barroque decoration, both on its exterior and inside, by the sculptor Jeroni Escarabatxeres.

It is worth going back a few metres to enter the **Barrio del Call★** (I, D2), the medieval Jewish ghetto, on the **Carrer Sant Domenec del Call,** in the old days called the Synagoga Mayor. This area was occupied by the Jews until they were finally expelled from Spain in the XV century. Within its walls there were schools, hospitals, baths, synagogues and even a university. Some of the noble houses that line this narrow street are evidence of the wealth that was accumulated in the Call. It is true that if you wish to appreciate their beauty you must stretch your neck considerably, since the only perspective possible is the verticle one.

The **house** at number 6 is particularly noteworthy. It is one of the oldest in the city, originally from the XII century. Once you are on

The narrow streets of the Gothic Quarter create a special atmosphere, with the light that can only be found in this Mediterranean city.

the Carrer del Call, one of the borders of the Jewish ghetto, you should continue along this street to the right while looking for the intersection with Carrer Banys Nous. This area has a markedly commercial character, once filled with stalls and shops of the Jews, and afterwards with shops selling silk and fashionable ladies' clothing. The **house** at number 14 has some interesting engravings in its plaster façade, unfortunately not in a very good state of repair. This house closes off Carrer Banys Nous. On this corner, once again outside the (today) imaginary line of the Roman wall, you should take Carrer Avinyó. This street's name was immortalized in one of

Picasso's paintings, inspired by the girls who worked in a brothel that seems to have been operating in the immediate area. Crossing the Carrer Ferran, you enter again the old fortified town on the Bajada de Sant Miguel, which harbours two fine pieces of architecture among its anodine buildings. On your left is the **Pasaje del Credit★★** (I, D2). The Parisian influence of the ironwork so popular at the time of its planning, in 1879, is more than evident. The famous painter Joan Miró was born and lived for many years in the house at number 4 on this street. To the right as you go up the Bajada de Sant Miguel you see the **Palau Centelles** (I, D2), built in

The Plaça de Sant Felip Neri, close to the Cathedral, is a quiet spot full of the splashing of its fountain's water.

El Call

The Jewish ghetto in Barcelona was the largest in all of Catalonia in the Middle Ages. Cited in the oldest surviving document from 1242, the Call (the word comes from Hebraic word "Qahal", which means assembly) was at that time merely a Jewish neighbourhood. Later it was made into a closed ghetto. It was built on the western part of the medieval city, within the Roman wall, between what is now the Palau de la Generalitat and the streets of Banys Nous and La Palla. Actually, there were two Jewish ghettos, separate but very near, called the Call Mayor and the Call Menor, or Call de Sanahuja. As the Jews played the role of intermediaries between the Catalan-Aragones monarchs and the Arabs, the Call became a place of wealth and learning. In it there were doctors, philosophers, poets, astrologists... and it had schools, a university, hospital and public baths. In August of 1391 the Call was attacked and burned during a revolt, and many of its inhabitants were killed. In 1492 the Jews were expelled from the kingdoms of Aragón and Castille. Today it is worthwhile visiting the streets of the Call, of Sant Domènec and Marlet, where the houses from the XII century are, possibly the oldest in the city.

1514 according to the norms of the Catalan Gothic. Despite the dominance of the Gothic at that time, some Renaissance motifs are visible in its sculpted ornamentation. On the corner by the palace turn to the right onto Carrer Gegants, which turns into Carrer de Palau, and then Carrer de Comtessa Sobradiel. All of this zone was occupied by the Palau Menor de Barcelona, a Medieval group of buildings that disappeared in 1857. Its owner, the countess for whom one of the streets is named, decided to have it torn down to make way for the dwellings that now occupy the site.

The Carrer Calella runs for only a

few metres until it finishes in the Plaça Regomir, the site of one of the four entrance gates into the Roman walled town. A street (which bears the names of Carrer Ciutat and Bisbe, what was once the Roman *decumanus)* sets out in a straight line to the gate at Plaça Nova, crossing all of the old town.

Your itinerary, however, continues along the narrow Carrer Cometa, which ends in the **Carrer Lledó★** (I, D2), an extremely interesting street somewhat similar to Carrer Montcada. It seems that at number 13 the poet Joan Boscán was born. He personally introduced Spanish literature to the Renaissance movement. Of the original building (demolished in 1873) hardly anything more than a few vestiges remain: a pair of Renaissance medallions on the nineteenth century façade, and part of the structure that was uncovered during a recent reform. At number 11 there is a strange patio beside the street through which you gain entrance to a huge **house** from the XVIII century. At numbers 7 and 4 there are Gothic-style houses with all of the typical features; door with voussoirs, patio with staircase, tower and verandah. The latter house was the residence of the counsellor Joan Fiveller, whose statue is on the façade of the building of the Ayuntamiento.

The Carrer Lledó runs into the Plaça Sant Just, clearly of funeral origins. A Gothic fountain with three spouts accentuates the peculiar atmosphere of this place. If you were able to elimi-nate the parked cars, the square would seem not to have entered the XX century. Obviously the square's most outstanding feature is its **Iglesia de los Santos Justo y Pastor ★** (I, D2), built between the XIV and XVI centuries. The church has a single nave with chapels located between its buttresses. Inside it there is an interesting **altarpiece** from the XVI century dedicated by Sant Feliu, the work of a Flemish sculptor. The Testamento Sacramental, a ceremony from the Middle Ages, is still practised in this chapel. Through this ceremony the people of Barcelona are able to arrange their last will and testament orally before going off on a trip. The presence of two witnesses makes the ceremony legally binding, if the case should arise that the party dies. If you go along the side of the church you will leave the square on the Carrer Hércules, named for the fellow who was supposed to have founded the city. At its intersection with Carrer Ciutat, going to the right you quickly reach the Plaça Sant Jaume. Right beside the **Carrer** Bisbe there is a little street called **Paradís★★** (I, D2), which goes to the oldest **remains** of the original Roman colony, the Corinthian columns of a temple dedicated to Augustus on top of *Mons Taber.* You can see these remains in the basement of the Gothic house that is the seat of the Centre Excursionista de Catalunya. Carrer Paradís goes directly towards the Cathedral, near where you began this itinerary of the Gothic Quarter.   ◆

The Eixample

- ❖ The Passeig de Gràcia and Vicinity
- ❖ The Carrer Mallorca and Passeig de Sant Joan
- ❖ The Sagrada Familia
- ❖ Avinguda Gaudí and Avinguda Diagonal
- ❖ Rambla de Catalunya

Between the XIII and XV centuries (the period of Barcelona's maximum economic and social splendour) the Roman wall began to get in the way of the city's expansion. While the citizens ran streets through the wall between towers, the medieval monarchs built their palaces on top of the robust Roman walls, and at the same time fortified the growing city with another wall, whose traces can followed through the present street plan on the Rondas de Sant Pau, Sant Antoni, Universitat and Sant Pere. These streets used to go round the medieval city.

Outside of these walls there was an expanse of cultivated land and a scattering of villages. This too can be seen in today's street

The rational monotony of El Eixample is relieved by the brilliance of the Sagrada Familia, the unfinished work of Antoni Gaudí.

plan, if you compare the width of the tangle of streets in these old centres of population (such as Gracia or Sant Andreu del Palomar) with those of the regular grid which was set up in the central area of the modern part of the city.

All of the area covered by the street grid, built up according to plan beginning in the last quarter of the nineteenth century, was given the name of Eixample (enlargement), a word used in the xix century in Barcelona and in other municipalities to denote urban growth planned to cope with the changes brought about by the industrial revolution. In Barcelona's case, this provisional name of technical derivation was never replaced by any other, perhaps due to its immediate acceptance by the people. The fact that the planned expansion of Barcelona was so innovative at that time, both in conception and scale, and that it was really a re-foundation of the city may also be at the root of the permanence of the name "Eixample". The story of the Eixample began when the government authorized the demolition of the medieval fortifications, which the municipal authorities began almost immediately thereafter, in the year 1854. That the authorities should have acted with such rapidity is a measure of how strongly felt was the desire (the need first became evident some ten years before) to be free of the stone corset which restricted the growth of the city's industries, and caused the overcrowding which led to the epidemic of plague at that time which killed so many people.

From the Sierra del Collserola, Barcelona appears like an immense grid stretching from the sea to Montjuïc mountain.

In El Eixample, even functional objects such as street lamps can become lovely urban decorational motifs.

The Eixample you see today gained its visual appeal from both the urban planners and the architects who worked on the project. On the one hand there was the plan of the engineer Ildefons Cerdà, pioneer in the science of "urbanization", as he used to like to call his business; and on the other hand was the Modernist movement in Catalonia, guided by the propositions of Gaudí, who was accompanied by a brilliant generation of architects, master-builders and craftsmen. Your tour of the Eixample should take into account these two facets of its interesting monuments.

❖ The Passeig de Gràcia and Vicinity★★ (II, C-B3)

Your itinerary through the Eixample begins in the heart of the old part of the city too, the Plaça Catalunya. But while the Ciutat Vella extends from this point towards the sea, and La Rambla is its spinal column, the new city grew in the direction of the mountain, on both sides of its main street, the Passeig de Gràcia. According to the peculiar system of directions used in Barcelona, the Eixample is divided into a right-hand part (dreta), and a left-hand (esquerra). A dry wash running down the Rambla de Catalunya that obstructed free passage between its one side to the other gave birth to this nomenclature. This geographical feature (which was not buried until the end of the past century) favoured the construction of more and higher quality buildings on the right-hand side, whose main street is the Passeig de Gràcia.

This boulevard runs along on top of the old route to what once was the village of Gràcia, today

"Si la Bossa Sona"

The people of Catalonia have a reputation for loving to count their money, and for being good businessmen. With regard to these matters, there are many jokes and stories told about them. Until a short time ago, the travelling salesmen that worked throughout Spain were all Catalans, and there were almost none of them in the army or the public administration.

Sayings such as "A Catalan could get bread from a stone" and "As it is in Sabadell, it is Dutch treat" are well known, but even better-known is the one about "Barcelona is good if your purse is full; but if it is full or empty, Barcelona is still good" (Barcelona és bona si la bossa sona; pero tant si sona com si no sona, Barcelona és bona). According to the expert in folklore, Joan Amades, the first part of the saying, known all over the Mediter-

ranean, is attributable to the Genovese, for whom Barcelona was good. Those from Pisa, who were not allowed to do business in the city, replied to the assertion of the Genovese with "if there is money in your purse", to which the Genovese terminated the discussion with "purse full or empty, it is still good". All in all, the saying seems to summarise perfectly the entrepreneurial spirit so characteristic of Barcelona, and today such a part of our human heritage.

absorbed by Barcelona, made another one of its quarters.

In the year 1827 this street began to be transformed into a place for strolling and relaxation. Not much more than the memory remains of the splendid gardens that flanked it, and the fountains whose murmur and song cheered it. Still the pavement is quite broad, and will allow you to discover lovely views in among the trees, the street-lamps, the buildings, the sky, and in the distance, the mountain of Tibadabo.

While you stroll, make sure to examine occasionally the pavement beneath you, doubtlessly one of the many luxuries that this promenade enjoys. Its hexagonal paving blocks create sinuous figures of many textures. They were designed by Gaudí for their manufacturer, Escofet, one of the companies that pioneered the fruitful collaboration of that time between industry and art.

At number 48 on Carrer Casp you find the first building that Gaudí designed in the Eixample, the **Casa Calvet** (I, B1) (1900), which blends in with the neighbouring houses. As is the case with the majority of Modernist buildings, it is a good idea to pay some attention to the **façade,** of course, but you should also keep in mind that one of the characteristics of the Modernist movement was the individual treatment of each and every constituent space. One of these spaces is the **vestibule.**

Once again on the promenade, the predominant style you will see on this first stretch is that of the Neogothic. Two especially representative buildings are the huge ones located at numbers 2-4, **Casa Pons y Pascual** (I, B1), 1891; and at number 6-14, **Casa Rocanova** (I, B1), 1917. Such recreations of historic styles characterize the first phase of Modernism. Neo-Orientalism also had many practitioners. At number 24 of the promenade there is, for example, a building of these characteristics which dates from 1899, although it has been partly mutilated. But the model that enjoyed the greatest prestige among architects and owners was the Gothic, a style charged with a wealth of meaning, associated as it was with the city's golden economic, political and social age. The desire to endow the new part of the city with a monumentality that was not to be found in the agricultural land on which it was to be built also contributed to the predilection for the Gothic.

The Modernist movement had a highly decorative character.

Crossing the Gran Via de les Corts Catalanes, take the turning to the right at the next street, the Carrer Diputació, which goes to the oldest part of the Eixample. When you reach the intersection with Carrer Pau Claris you will find yourself facing the first block

A mirror's reflection can never substitute for reality, but sometimes it can create beautiful aesthetic effects.

of the grid, that was completely built up only ten years after the medieval walls were knocked down. It is the one that is bounded by the streets of Diputació, Consell de Cent, Roger de Llúria, and Pau Claris, and is divided lengthwise by the passatge Permanyer, which begins at number 114 of the Pau Claris Street.

The design of Cerdà for the restructuring and broadening of Barcelona was approved by the central government in 1860, but not by the local powers. This circumstance created a lot of controversy and even ill will towards the urban planner, which continued unabated for decades. This is perhaps the explanation for the little enthusiasm shown for the

Modernist façades are to be seen everywhere in Barcelona.

urban planning of Cerdà. In fact, of his original plan only the part that the central government promoted and that which stubbornly insisted on the planting of trees (and the concommitant width of the pavement) has been respected. The real-estate speculation of the people of Barcelona did away with the rest.

The most relevant aspects of Cerda's urban plan can be resumed in two ideas. First of all there is the ideal of the rectangular grid, into which the perimeter of the old city was to be integrated as well. The grid was to have 60 city blocks parallel to the shoreline and 20 blocks known as "islands" on the perpendicular. Within this immense mesh Cerdà planned a rational distribution of services (a social centre every four blocks, a market every twelve...) in an attempt to avoid the setting up of hierarchies among the urban neighbourhoods (an aim the owners of the land did not share). That is to say, he intended to create an egalitarion city, in keeping with the best socialist utopic traditions. Today you can see from a map that the plan for a street grid has been complied with in two thirds of the area, although the space reserved for services has hardly been respected. The second basic idea is that of the city block, a new idea at that time introduced by Cerdà. He planned them as square islands with their corners truncated to leave triangular spaces. The idea behind these truncations was the increase in visibility at intersections thus achieved. Cerdà planned that of the four sides of each block, only two would be built up, while two would be left for parks and gardens. You will notice that not one of the blocks of the Eixample was constructed as was so generously planned by the engineer. Recently the demolition of some buildings has left room for an attempt at the original idea of Cerdà, at the intersection of Carrer Marina and Carrer Indústria (a bit of a distance from your itinerary), where they have planted the garden Jardí de la Industria.

On your stroll through the Passatge Permanyer you can mull over the contrast between the most characteristic features of Cerda's urban planning and what actually exists. This stretch of road is the intermediate link between the original idea and the end result, after the passing of some decades. Once they had put up two of the sides of this particular "island", permission was granted for the construction of single-family dwellings in the rest of the space. The tranquility and colour their vegetation provide give you a slight idea of the potential effect of Cerda's solution to Barcelona's housing problems, had it been implemented. The **Passatge Permanyer**★★ (II, B3-4) runs into the Carrer Roger de Llúria. At number 56 on this street there is a tunnel bearing the inscription "Manantial del agua de la asociación de Propietarios" (fountain belonging to the owners) which serves as an entrance to the gardens **Jardines Torre de les Aigües.** Your visit to the garden will afford you the opportunity to see the interior of a typical city block in the Eixample.

Torre de les Aigües, new ideas for old structures.

The rear face of these magnificent buildings usually is composed of a group of uninteresting arcades, and what you see of them is largely panes of glass and wooden panels supported by metal beams. On seeing them, Le Corbusier proposed that these interior structures, so stylized and pure, be the model for the main façades of the buildings.

Once again on the Carrer Llúria, at its intersection with Carrer Consell de Cent, you will find the first group of dwellings built in Eixample, on three of the four corners. Houses lacking artistic relief, they are typical of the model that was used throughout the grid. The typical house of the Eixample was planned by Cerdà to be a miniature city, or even the "urbe originaria". Perhaps the

Casa Batllo, an example of the genius of Antoni Gaudí.

most representative feature of these common houses of that period is the functional distribution of the balconies, which soon replaced the windows in a symmetrical façade between dividing walls. There was usually a "main" floor at the level of the first storey, the one called "principal", where the owner of the building lived. In many buildings in Eixample the hierarchy of storeys is perceptible. The lower floors were endowed with decoration, while the upper floors completely lacked any symbol of prestige. This situation was reversed when lifts were installed in these buildings. These characteristics can be seen in hundreds of blocks of dwellings which, besides displaying this common hierarchy of storeys, also bear some artistic imprint. To see some

of them it is best to return along the Carrer Consell de Cent to the Passeig de Gràcia, and cross it on the pedestrian walk. You will then find yourself before one of the most typical "islands" of the Eixample, the one known as the **Block of Discord★★** (II, B3). Its façade, which borders the street for 113 m, constitutes a veritable little museum of Modernist architecture. The five buildings that make up the block not only incorporate the artistic lines most typical of the period, but four of them also bear the signature of the most brilliant architects of that period. And they also have another factor in common, being the four of them the result of artistic reforms of pre-existing common buildings. Looking in the direction of the mountain, the first building is the **Casa Lleó Morera** (II, B3) (1906), the work by Lluis Domènech i Montaner (1849-1923). He was the author of other such noble buildings as the Palau de Música, and a principal figure of the Modernist movement in Catalonia.

Within this movement there were two marked artistic lines. One tended towards expressionism and the absurd, typified by the work of the genius Gaudí, while the other inclined towards a certain rationalism and spatial order (in spite of its floral whims), typified by the work of Domènech i Montaner, who was also a genius. The business premises of this building were barbarously mutilated in 1934, when Noucentisme was triumphing in its efforts to extirpate all trace of Modernism from the Eixample.

Modernists were especially interested in the use of multi-coloured stained glass, like that in the Casa Lleó Morera de Domènech i Montaner.

The Fundació Tàpies, a diaphanous space in which to contemplate the unrivalled work of an artist from the world vanguard.

Make every effort to see the profusion of ornamentation that decorates and beautifies its **vestibule** and its **staircase.** The decoration of the façade next door is the work by Enric Sagnier, who designed it in 1910 on a reformed, previously-existing structure. The work of Sagnier shines in the Eixample more for its fecundity than for its artistic merit. He was the favourite architect of the high bourgoisie. Within the Modernist movement his work represents the least innovative line, the one most open to Viennese influence.

At number 41 is the splendid **Casa Amatller** (II, B3) (1900), designed by Josep Puig i Cadalfalch (1867-1957). The building has an air about it of a Gothic house with Catalan and also Flemish features, of which its enormous fronton with stairs is outstanding. As is evident from an inspection of the work, the most highly-skilled craftsmen of that time collaborated on the project. Sharing the dividing wall is the **Casa Batlló** (II, B3) (1906), also the product of the reform of a previously-existing building. The unmistakable imprint of Gaudí (1852-1926) is visible in its every corner. While every one of the building's features is a prodigy of artistic elaboration, the sculptural treatment of the main rostrum and the polychromic detail of the façade (which tends to erase the dividing line between the interior and the exterior of the house) are particularly outstanding. The solution provided by the tower and cupola of the house, in an attempt to harmonize it with the neighbouring Casa Amatller, is also brilliant.

When you come to the wide Carrer Aragó, turn to the left and go on for a few metres to visit the **Fundació Tàpies★** (II, C3) at number 25. The building was originally the headquarters of the publisher Editorial Montaner y Simón. This work by Lluis Domènech i Montaner (1880), along with that of Vicens de Gaudí, is ususally considered to mark the starting point of Catalan Modernism. After it was reformed it was crowned with a piece of statuary, the *Núvol i Cadira* (cloud and chair) by Antoni Tàpies, which has aroused quite a bit of controversy. On the corner of the next cross-street, at number 66 of the promenade, there is an interesting example of a medieval reproduction which was so popular in its time. This **Casa Marfà** (II, B3) was built in 1906.

At the intersection with Carrer Mallorca there is a fine Neogothic building, perfectly restored and made into a hotel, that was built in 1891 by Vilaseca (1848-1910), a Modernist architect of some importance. He also was responsible for the Arc del Triomf (1888). On the next city block is the jewel of the greatest worth, among the many in the grid, the **Casa Milà★★** (II, B3), known as "La Pedrera". Designed by Gaudí in 1905, the work was finished five years later. But one year before it was finished it was granted the status of a monument, which allowed it to slightly excede the normal limits established by municipal building codes of that time. Gaudí poured all of his creative genius into this block of dwellings, the last one of its kind that he was to build. The building occupies one entire corner in the

The Casa Milà might be the masterpiece of Gaudí, where he brought together such inherently different materials as iron and stone.

Eixample, and shows off an imposing **façade** made of stone so molded and apparently ductile that it appears to be made of clay. Especially beautiful is the ornamentation of the **balconies,** of an expressionism and liberty of imagination without architectural precedent. On the flat roof of "La Pedrera", planned to be a viewpoint, Gaudí erected a series of enigmatic sculptures to form a veritably fantastic landscape. Like all the other Modernist architects, Gaudí was attentive to every single artistic detail.

On the same side of the Passeig de Gràcia there is another building of interest, what was the home of the Modernist painter Ramon Casa, at number 96 on the street, built in 1899. The painter's dwelling , with its lovely coffered cieling and huge fireplace, is open to visitors. It is on the first floor, entering through a shop that sells furniture and domestic appliances on the ground floor.

❖ The Carrer Mallorca and Passeig de Sant Joan

At the next intersection your itinerary leaves the promenade, turning to the right on Carrer Rosello, and turns to the right again on Carrer Pau Claris until you come to Carrer Mallorca, two streets further down. You turn left onto it. Unlike the case of the Ciutat Vella, where the street names vividly reflect historical events, the nomenclature that was applied to the streets of the grid of Eixample was the fruit of global planning. It seems that the new residents began complaining about the lack of street names in

The figures dotting the flat roof of the Casa Milà create a really strange, enigmatic space.

their newly built neighbourhoods, and instigated City Hall to do something about it. As a result one of the city's chroniclers, Victor Balaguer, was hired to draw up a list of appropriate names. Balaguer discharged his responsiblity by proposing names taken from the history of Catalonia, selected from among its most important events; names of territories such as Valencia and Mallorca, which used to belong to it; its national institutions, such as the Diputació and Consell de Cent; and illustrious names from the fields of politics and art, such as Roger de Llúria and Ausiàs March.

On the stretch of Carrer Mallorca that makes up part of this itinerary, until the Passeig de Sant Joan, you can see two buildings that clearly bear the mark of the architect Domènech. The first, the **Palau Montaner** (II, B3) (1893), is at the intersection with Carrer Roger de Llúria. Its cornice is decorated with outstanding ceramic tile. Across the street from it is the small palace which today is used as the seat of the Colegio de Abogados. Both are fine examples from the early days of Eixample, before the single-family dwellings (some even of artistic interest) of the well-to-do disappeared, to be replaced almost in their entirety by blocks of dwellings. The second building by Domènech i Montaner is the Neogothic **Casa Thomas** (II, B3) (1898), located at number 291 on this street. It is also an example of the buildings that should have been built in the Eixample, and were not. Domènech built the two lower floors, one a workshop

Glorieta of the Casa Marfa, from the beginnings of this century.

and the other a dwelling. In 1912 new floors were added, and the towers of the original project were made into rostrums, while the original style of the building was generally respected. Unfortunately, this case is nearly unique in Eixample, as the majority of the enlargements carried out after the city building codes were changed to allow higher buildings were enlargements that mutilated the original decoration and ignored questions of style and character. In addition to being the site of these two artistically interesting buildings, Carrer Mallorca is also flanked by various houses, built by anonymous architects, that bear the stamp of the Modernist movement, so popular among the builders of the "dreta" of Eixample. The

Plaça Mossèn Jacint Verdeguer is at the intersection of two of the city's great avenues, the Avinguda Diagonal, which traverses Cerda's grid on the diagonal, as its name indicates, and the Passeig de Sant Joan. A statue of the illustrious Catalan poet, Verdaguer, presides over the square from atop its monumental column.

You should be sure to visit the rooms of the **Palau Macaya★** (II, A4) (1901), at number 108 of Passeig de Sant Joan. It is a stately home, built by Puig i Cadalfach, which today houses a foundation that is important to Barcelona. Its rooms are open to visitors. The work of Puig i Cadalfach is characterized by his careful treatment of his interior spaces, as well as his Neoclassical tastes.

❖ The Sagrada Familia★★ (II, A4)

Continuing along the Carrer Mallorca for another three city blocks, you will be surprised by the imposing towers of the **Temple Expiatori de la Sagrada Familia,** the most ambitious work by Gaudí and emblematic of the city, known the world over. When Antoni Gaudí took over the project for building a new cathedral in Barcelona in 1883, he was barely thirty years old. In 1926, when a tram car mortally injured him at the intersection of the streets Gran Via and Bailén, after forty years of work, the architect had seen only one of the side towers of the eastern façade finished. It and the wall of the apse were the only parts of the church that were being worked on at that time. Effectively, the Sagrada Familia was a life's work, or of several lives, for if what was built under his direction is spectacular, then what remains in his sketches and notes, a project that overflows from the heights of architectural ambition, is doubly so. The

---

Symbols

There are many mystical figures, patrons, symbols and mascots associated with Barcelona. According to legend the city was founded by Hercules, the hero who sent his ships over the Mediterranean, who fell in love with the site of Barcelona, called barca nova, *and changed himself into the mountain of Montjuïc to be able to take care of it. The city's patron saints are the Roman Eulalia, a girl from Sarrià, who died a virgen and martyr; and the Virgen de la Merced, who was the patron saint of the Order of the Mercedes, whose job it was to ransom captive Christians from the Moors. There are two sculpted figures which are both considered to be the symbol of Barcelona. One is the lady with an umbrella in the Parque de la Ciutadella, and the other is* La Dama i l'Ocell, *in the Parque de l'Escorxador. But there are the following things that might also be considered characteristic of the city. There is La Rosa de Fuego, anarchiustic; the well-known Monumento a Colón; the Sagrada Familia, by the Modernist architect Gaudí; the albino gorilla Copito de Nieve; the three chimney stacks of El Parelelo; and the Palacio Nacional de Montjuïc, which houses the Museo de Arte de Cataluña.*

The outline of the slender towers of the Sagrada Família has become one of the most well-known symbols of the City of the Count.

layout is in the typical form of a cross, exactly as the first architect of the project had planned. This architect had in mind building a Neogothic church, a faithful reproduction of those from the Ogival period, complete with all their characteristic features. Gaudí's genius resides in his having done exactly the opposite, for even though he accepted the aesthetic code of the Gothic, he knew how to surpass it by alteration, combination and reformulation. He thus created a new style, intimately linked with the tastes of his time, and highly creative.

On each of the arms of the cross **façades** have been built. The façade of the **Nacimiento** is to the east, and that of the **Pasión** is to the west, the only ones built up to this date. There was a third façade, the façade of the **Gloria,** planned for the southern side, the main entrance to the church. The central nave was to be crowned by an immense cupola that Gaudí wished to be 70 m high, surrounded by five more towers, symbolic of the Virgen and the four Evangelists. If you think of adding the cupola and five towers to the 107 metre-high tower that already has been built, you get an idea of the grandiose size of the original project. In the Sagrada Familia that you have today, if you are interested in seeing the part that Gaudí was responsible for, look then at the crypt, the wall of the apse and the door of the Nacimiento. What has been built since the time of Gaudí came under the direction of a group of architects who have tried to interpret the complicated

models and confusing drawings left by their inspired creator. The arguments about whether or not the construction project should be continued have reached the point of degeneration into bitterness. It is difficult to reconcile those who argue for the project's continuation with those opposed. But what is certainly true is that the part done by Gaudí affords the onlooker a lively dialogue covering his architectural evolution, his amazing formal discoveries and, finally, the development of his artistc thought over the course of his lifetime. If you are sharp-eyed you will be able to distinguish the various stages of Gaudí's development, in the form of stratum that testify to the different periods of Gaudí's professional career, first of all, but also to those of the Modernist movement in general. Hence the crypt and the apse show the Neogothic influence of Gaudí's beginnings; although the ornamentation of a naturalist variety (vegetal forms and animal shapes carved in the stone) were the result of an unexpected twist in this style. The naturalist sculptures are repeated in the portico of the Nacimiento, but there are also symbolic and deliquescent shapes that culminate in the slender sculpture of the tower and their polychromed pinnacles, a wonder of geometric beauty. The continuation of the work, however, lacks artistic fire, due to the use of static, or in some cases, non-existant, plans. Between 1953 and 1976 the towers of the façade of the Pasión were built, in an imitation of Gaudí's style. Their ornamentation is being

The Avinguda Gaudí begins at the foot of the Sagrada Familia and ends at the doors of the Modernist Hospital de Sant Pau.

sculpted by Subirachs, as the result of an effort to involve an artist directly in the construction again. The work on the façade of the Gloria and the roofing of the central nave is going ahead, following the original plans and studies left by Gaudí. Your visit to the site will include the added attraction of a lift to the top of the four eastern towers to a viewpoint at an elevation of 60 m, from where you get a wonderful panoramic view of the city.

❖ Avinguda Gaudí and Avinguda Diagonal

The Avinguda Gaudí begins across the street from the Sagrada Familia, and goes to the main gate of the **Hospital de Sant Pau** (1912), a project designed by Domènech i Montaner. The orientation of the street is radically opposed to the Cerda's plan, whom he detested. In fact this avenue is the only remaining vestige of the urban planning done by the Frenchman León Jaussely, who in the first decade of this century was to set about modifying the main lines of Eixample. The political instability of those years made the execution of his plan inviable. The Avinguda Gaudí divides four blocks of the grid. Setting off along it, at the first of these you can turn to your left onto the Carrer Rosselló and continue along until you reach the Avinguda Diagonal. This point is dominated by another unique building, the **Casa Terrades** (1905), known to the townsfolk as the **Casa de les Punxes★** (II, B3) (house of points), a magnificent job by Puig i Cadafalch which takes up a complete irregularly-shaped block, transected by the Avinguda Diagonal. Standing

The Casa de les Punxes is reminiscent of a Medieval palace.

out from among its Neogothic features is its wealth of ornamentation, the work of highly-skilled craftsmen, as well as the bare brickwork (at that time it was the custom to cover brickwork with a veneer of stone) which explores this material's immense decorative possibilities.

On the other side of the Avinguda Diagonal, at number 373, is another building by the same architect, the **Palau Quadras★★** (II, B3) (1904), today used as the seat of the **Museo de la Música.** As with so many stately buildings of the period, the work was inspired by the Gothic palaces of Barcelona. At the end of this block there is an obelisque that marks the intersection of the Avinguda Diagonal with Passeig de Gràcia.

❖Rambla de Catalunya

The Rambla de Catalunya runs parallel to Passeig de Gracia through Eixample. The boulevard with its leafy central promenade links up with La Rambla in the Plaça Catalunya. The noble buildings that flank the boulevard, along with the interesting shops of the area, make the propositon of walking its entire length to the very beginning of the Ciutat Vella an inviting one. At the intersection with Avinguda Diagonal there is the **Casa Serra** (II, B3), a fine example of the harmonization in an urban context of Modernist styles with mordern architectural practices. It was built in 1908 by Puig i Cadalfach, to be the property and seat of the Diputació Provincial, for whom the glass and metal building that frames the

The edifice of the Universidad de Barcelona, a work from the last century, and a reminder of the rich medieval past of the city.

view of the palace was built recently. Along the length of the Rambla de Catalunya there are interesting Modernist buildings. What follows is a list of their street number, year of construction, and in some cases, the architect responsible: 125 (1900); 122 (1904); 115 (actually the Gothic parish church **Iglesia de Sant Ramon de Penyafort** (II, B3), moved to its present location in 1880 from the site of its construction); 112 (1900); 104 (Sagnier, 1894); 103 (1903); 101 (1905); 96 (Sagnier, 1902 "this is a clearly an example of the barbarities perpetuated after the height of buildings was allowed to be increased"); 88 (1906); 92-94 (1898); 86 (1899); 78 (1909); 76 (1915); 74 (1909); 72 (1892); 54 (Vilaseca, 1903); 47 (Sagnier, 1904); (Some of the city's most prestigious art galleries are to be found on Carrer Consell de Cent, here to the left. Continuing along on the Rambla de Catalunya); 33 (Sagnier, 1891); 27 (1902); 25 (1894); 23 (1895); 19 (1909); and 17 (Vilaseca, 1896).

Once you reach the Gran Via de les Corts Catalanes you can turn to the left to visit, on the next block, the **Universitat de Barcelona** (II, C3), a Medievalist construction directed by Elias Rogent between the years 1860 and 1870. Romanesque features are modernized in the building. Especially attractive are its two cloisters, the Claustro de Letras and the Claustro de Ciencias. From the Plaça Universitat you should take the Carrer Pelai, full of shops, that runs on into the heart of the city, the beginning and the end of your tour of the Eixample. ◆

Olympic Barcelona (Montjuïc and the Vila Olímpica)

The transformation of the old Barcelona was visibly reflected in the construction and reinforcing of its walls by the Romans. Later, after their demolition in 1854, the growth of the city entered a dynamically opposed stage. Where once the unitary style of the Gothic house, limited architectural imagination and a love of the unchangable over time prevailed, the new period was characterized by the use of a variety of styles, a spreading out in space, and the previously inconceivable notion of the city's unlimited expansion. The framework for this re-founding of the modern Barcelona was the rationalist urban design of Ildefons Cerdà, who laid out the Eixample. The execution of Cerda's plan was anything but continu-ous; it was subject to the ups and downs which accompanied alternating economic crisis and bonanzas. At certain times, nevertheless, Barcelona's develop-ment has recieved an over-whelming boost, with attendant cityfying of new (previously) out-lying space, improvements in surface transport systems and monumental projects. These periods in its recent history have coincided with events in the city that caused intense enthusiasm, such as the Exposición Interna-cional in 1888, the Exposición Internacional in 1929 and the Olympic Games in 1992. The major urban renovation brought about as a consequence of the two expositions (in the area of La Ciutadella and in the Plaça Espa-nya, respectively) were absorbed

A la Avenida del Marqués de Comillas

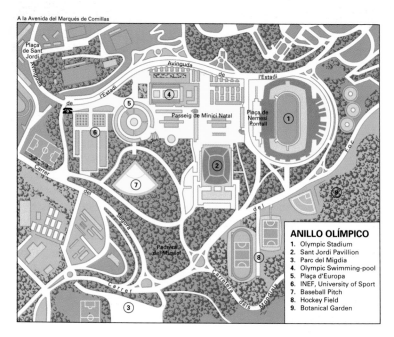

ANILLO OLÍMPICO

1. Olympic Stadium
2. Sant Jordi Pavillion
3. Parc del Migdia
4. Olympic Swimming-pool
5. Plaça d'Europa
6. INEF, University of Sport
7. Baseball Pitch
8. Hockey Field
9. Botanical Garden

Ordered rows of street lamps lead along the Avenida de la Reina María Cristina to the monumental Palau Nacional.

Today's stadium retains the façade of the old one, as a symbol of the long-standing desire of Barcelona's citizens to host the Olympic Games.

and digested long ago. The immediacy of the third of these historic events, however, allows you to contemplate its impact on this new Barcelona stirred up by the Olympic boost.

Barcelona's face was modified to an extraordinary extent in those years that preceeded the opening of the Games in 1992. The highway system has been improved with the addition of two new urban motorways, the Segon Cinturó (Second Belt Road) and the Cinturó Litoral (Shore Belt); public spaces have been reserved for the use of the citizens (parks, sports centres, shopping centres); tremendous projects such as the Torre de Comunicaciones in Collserola have been carried out; and some of the neighbour-hoods have been given a face-lift, especially those most neglected

in Ciutat Vella. But most of all, the Olympic torch has burned brightest in the two areas of the mountain of Montjuïc and along the sea-front. In the former area the major sports facilities for the event have been built, and in the latter a new city within the city has been created.

❖ Montjuïc★★

The origin of the "City of the Count" is even more closly linked with this promontory (191 m high, rising majestically in the south of the city) that divides the coastline in two, than with the flatland through which Barce-lona now spreads.

The first Iberic colonizers, the mythic Laietanos (who left little more than their coins bearing the name *Laiesken,* apparently that of their pre-Romanic settlement) settled on top of this privileged enclave that overlooks the mouths of the Llobregat and Besós Rivers. The mountain's present name doubtlessly comes from "Mount of the Jews", clearly referring to the Hebrew necropolis that once existed on the mountain's slope. The construction of modern urban neighbourhoods began on its northern slope at the time of the Exposición Internacional in 1929. Today it is the home of the premises of the Feria Internacional de Muestras, between the Plaça Espanya and the Palau Nacional (the latter is the seat of the **Museu d'Arte de Catalunya)** (II, F2). In this area there are illuminated **fountains** and cascades, the artistic invention of the engineer Carles Buigas; and the pavillion **Pabellón de Alemania,** from the exposition of 1929, the work of Mies Vam der Rohe, reconstructed from the plans of the one that was torn down after the Exposición had concluded.

As you go climbing up the mountain on Avinguda del Marqués de Comillas you will be surprised to discover a faithful reproduction of the gate of San Vicent from the wall of Ávila. Passing through the gate you will be even more surprised by the reproductions of typical quarters and the monuments of each of the regions of Spain. This is the **Poble Espanyol** (II, F1), today an area of exciting nightspots.

It is worthwhile visiting the bar set up in the simulated gate of Ávila. It contains furniture imaginatively designed by Mariscal, also the author of the 1992 Olympic mascot-logo, the charming dog called Cobi.

The Palau d'Esports Sant Jordi is the most innovative work in the Anella Olimpica, built according to the design of the Japonese Arata Isozaki.

El Pueblo Español is a homage to vernacular architecture.

From the height of the promontory in **Castell de Montjuïc** (II, F3), you will have a view of the entire city and the port. The castle was a military bastion erected in the XVI century which has played a decisive, sometimes traumatic, role in the history of the city. Today it is a splendid vantage point, and has been since its military usefulness came to an end in 1940. The display rooms of the **Museo del Ejército** are the last remains of its old military functions.

A good part of the mountain which had not been previously been built on has been used as a location for a sports city, directly as a result of the hosting of the Olympic Games in 1992. This sports complex (Anell Olimpic) is the site of some major building projects. In the first place, there is the outstanding **Estadi Olimpic** (II, F2). The façade of a previously-existing stadium was incorporated into the new stadium, as a symbol of the length of time that the people of Barcelona have been waiting to host the Olympic Games. The floor of the old stadium was lowered by 11 metres. Its race track has nine 400 metre long lanes, with a great expanse of lawn in the centre. It has seating capacity for a crowd of 55,000 spectators, with good visiblity from all seats. For the main tribune a 150 metre long by 30 metre wide projecting platform has been designed. The door of this tribune is presided over by a sculptural work by Pau Gargallo, also recycled from the original stadium.

The most imposing work of the complex is doubtlessly the **Palau d'Esports Sant Jordi** (1985-1990), built according to an innovative design by the Japanese architect Arata Isozaki. Its covering is also outstanding, the work of the engineer Mamoru Kawaguchi, made up of a complex, curving, metallic network that supports its panels and roof tiles. The local people imagine a sleeping dragon when they see the profile of the roof structure. Perhaps it is the dragon that traditionally accompanied Sant Jordi (Saint George). If the pavillion is a wonder of the latest architecture and engineering feats, then its entrances are completely up to the work's high calibre. In front of the Palace of Sant Jordi there is a grand esplanade with a lake and a beautiful group of oriental sculptures, the work of Aiko Mijawaki, the wife of Isozaki.

From the doors of the Palau Nacional one can contemplate the Plaça de Espanya, flanked by its two towers; in the background is Monte Tibidabo.

All in all, it does not seem out of place to predict that the Palacio de Deporte de Sant Jordi will serve to keep alive the memory of the 1992 Olympic Games for years and years into the future. At the foot of the Stadium and the Sports Palace the architect from Barcelona, Ricardo Bofill, has built another notable edifice, the **Universitat del Esport,** with a Neoclassic façade that evokes the Greek origins of the Games. The **Parc del Migdia** completes the Olympic premises. It is a botanical and forest garden in which is preserved the outdoor environment of the mountain, its major attraction since the city was born.

❖ The Olympic Village

The people of Barcelona often have complained that their city lives with its back turned to the Mediterranean Sea. Effectively, what with the harbour ware-houses and equipment, the rail-way and port industries, the port was cut off from the aver-age resident in the flatlands, its influence unfelt. Perhaps the most spectacular of all the initia-tives that have been taken with the date of the opening of the Olympics in mind is the urban renewal project that is reforming the harbour area of the city. The regeneration of its beaches, the creation of an enormous park running along the entire length of the seashore, and the con-struction of a garden city over-looking the sea are the highlights of this program to create the New Barcelona. The village which will be the Olympic residence during the games has emblem-atic buildings in the form of two skyscrapers of different architec-

It is a peculiar sight one gets of the city while suspended from the cables of the aerial tramway that climbs up Montjuïc mountain.

tural styles, which look like two fabulous city guards there in the harbour area. The first one you will encounter, if you come from the harbour or from the Ciutat Vella, is the **Hotel Arts** (II, B6). Its steel framework is visible in its façade. The second one is the **Torre Mapfre** (II, B6), with its glass-covered façade. Both buildings are 44 storeys high, 153.5 m in all, and hence the tallest buildings in Spain. At their base is a monumental square, as well as a quarter called Nova Icaria, named in remembrance of the seafront neighbourhood that was here before the area was taken over by industrial operations. The area that has been recovered for dwellings spreads out over a surface area equal to that of 50 of the blocks of the Eixample. Each new city block was designed by a different group of architects. Thus the Olympic Village has among its authors not only the most renowned Spanish architects (such as Federico Correa, Alfonso Milà, Óscar Tusquets, Ricard Bofill, Albert Viaplana and Helio Piñón), but also architects of international renown (such as the Portuguese Alvaro Siza Vieira, author of the Centro Meteorológico). Some visually attractive industrial features have been left as reminders of the recent past of these lands.

Hence you see the water towers of Macosa company, and nineteenth century smokestacks there. The concept of integrated dwellings, services, gardens, recreational facilities and access points make this Olympic Village an example for cities of the future to follow.   ◆

Unique Quarters and other Points of interest

❖ Gràcia
❖ La Barceloneta and the Parc de la Ciutadella
❖ Barcelona's Squares and Parks
❖ The Nou Barris
❖ The Monasterio de Pedralbes
❖ Tibidabo

❖ The Quarter of Gràcia (II, B1)

One of the objectives of the urban plan drawn up by Ildefons Cerdà for the Eixample was the improvement of the surface transport network connecting the different communities scattered about the flatland. But when the plan was put into effect, the unexpected growth in population brought about the absorption of several communities that had previously been independent; from 1897 on, these communities became part of the city of Barcelona. This absorption considerably enriched Barcelona, since not only were the communities' streets joined to those of the city, but also the historical towns, with their peculiar characteristics, merged with that of the city. From among the villages and hamlets that have become neighbourhoods of Barcelona, such as Horta, Sarrià, Sant Andreu del Palomar, and Sant Martí dels Provençals, the most outstanding is the old village of Gràcia, which still preserves its uniqueness.

The community of Gràcia originated at the intersection of two grand Roman roads. One of them came from Las Galias (what is today the street Travessera de Gràcia), and the other linked Barcelona with Sant Cugat (Passeig and Major de Gràcia).

The community's name comes from a monastery founded in the Middle Ages, dedicated to Santa María de Gràcia.

As a matter of fact, until the XVII century there were only ecclesiatical buildings and agricultural land in the area. Craftsmen and farm labourers settled in the area

Popular art as seen in one of the streets of the Barrio de Gracia.

afterwards, with the nearby Barcelona constricted by medieval walls contributing mightily to its growth, as more and more people came looking for space to live in.

The most brilliant period in its history occurred in the second half of the XIX century. At that time workers', anarchists' and revolutionaries' groups established themselves in Gràcia. Its squares were the scene of more than one demonstration, and its two markets are called Llibertat (liberty) and Revolució (revolution). The former still keeps its name. Today you will see that the neighbourhood of Gràcia still is unique, the home for some particular groups of people, such as the Catalan gypsies. The atmosphere in the area is generally very tranquil, as its streets are made, made to the measure of its people, suspicious of and aloof from the urban whirlwinds that blow around it.

The regular grid of the Eixample covers a good part of the centre of Gràcia, although you will quickly notice the differences between the width and layout of the streets, from one housing tract to another. In spite of the narrowness of its streets, and their labyrinthine layout, Gràcia is especially appealing to the people of Barcelona. For one thing it has squares throughout it, something that the central part of the city is lacking, as a result of a "perverse" interpretation of Cerda's grid.

Such squares as Plaça del Sol, Raspall, Ruis i Taulet and Virreina make up part of the city's emotional substrate, even though

The decorative features of the Modernist movement are everywhere in the Gràcia quarter, as in all the urban area of Barcelona.

they are not very large. In 1985 the Plaça del Sol was remodeled, marking the beginning of a renewal process carried out in the quarter, primarily through the introduction of more space for pedestrians. There is a tower more than 30 metres high in the Plaça Rius i Taulet. It is crowned by a clock and belfry. This tower was erected in 1862, in compliance with the norm that the City Hall had to have a clock in front of it (usually it was the clock of a church).

Of the various convents and monasteries that existed in the area, the Barroque **Iglesia de los Josepets** is still standing. It was built in 1626 by the Carmelites. It is on the corner of the square that the city dedicated to Ferdinand de Lesseps, who was the French counsellor in Barcelona.

The quality of the architecture of Gracia is uneven. There are some interesting Modernist buildings, and other eclectic ones less so. But its main attraction is doubtlessly the impression that Gaudí left on it, for in Gràcia is the pioneer building of Modernism, and also the first of Gaudí's prolific career. On its outskirts he designed a fantastic residential area that today is known as the **Park Güell.**

The **Casa Vicens** (II, A2), is located on the Carrer Colinas, a little cross street that links Carrer Gran de Gràcia with the Avinguda del Princep de Asturies. The house is considered to be the opera prima of the Catalan Modernist movement (so also is the building of Editorial Montaner i Simón, by Domènech). The project dates from 1878, although its construction was not finished until almost a decade later. This little palace-residence, once in the middle of a splendid garden, is of an orientalist style, a style much in vogue at that time. Nevertheless, Gaudí's contribution was his very personal interpretation of the Neomudéjar style, an imaginative prelude to Modernism.

As was to become the rule, this first house of Vicens attracted the attention of the experts, due to the architectural solutions that derived from a special conception of space. It also caught the eye of lovers of art, above all because of its exuberant ornamental work, in this case the plastic play between ceramic tile and stone, and the expresive strength of the iron gratings of its fence and windows.

A ceramic medallion at the main entrance to the **Park Güell★★,** on Carrer Olot, bears the English word "Park" rather than the Spanish "Parque", or Catalan "Parc", because its promotor, Güell, (as well as its architect, Gaudí), wished its name to reflect the efforts they had made in building their residential area on the slopes of a hill on the flatland of Barcelona. They wanted the name to reflect the tranquility of their garden-housing tract away from the hubbub of the city, but located conveniently nearby, in the style of the ones built in England during the XIX century. Of the 60 lots that were put up for sale, aimed at a potential market of well-off families in Barcelona looking for a permanent residence, only three were built on. If you subtract the houses Güell and Gaudí had built for themselves, the scale of the business disaster becomes clear. This same complete failure, in financial terms, however, has provided the inhabitants of the city with an expanse of parkland where they have enjoyed, since 1922, the leafy forest setting that Gaudí designed for the entrances and service installations of the housing tract. This city-garden was conceived of as an enclosed, protected space, with a wall around its entire perimetre. In imitation of the medieval architecture, two pavillions like fortified towers were erected at the sides of the main entrance. In one of them the watchman lived, and in the oth-

er a reception area was set up. The roof of both buildings is a spectacular covering of ceramic tiles, an anticipation of the *collage,* or *trencadís* technique, which employed irregular pieces of ceramic tile. You see this feature used in ornamentation all over the park.

Gaudí was a brilliant, original interpreter of natural forms, to which he gave special importance. In the main entrance there are two fine examples of his interpretative abilities; one is the group of mushrooms that culminate the roof of the pavillions, in the form of a cupola; and the other is the multicolour salamander that divides the main staircase in two. Here you have an example of the integration of the arts of painting, sculpture

A salamander welcomes you at the entrance to the Park.

The precious technique of El Trencadis *in a detail of a bench.*

and architecture, to which Modernism aspired.

The central area of the garden is the site of two squares of a most improbable design. The first is a hall of columns that supports a part of the second, roofless one. The 96 columns used in the first square have Doric features conveniently altered, combined and definitively transformed. The square was originally planned to be the market area of the housing tract. This use of architectural features outside of their normal context was to become one of the most innovative features of Gaudí's art.

The portentous colonnade terminates in a sort of cornice of sinuous shape, decorated with multicoloured ceramic tile. The sinuosity is nothing other than the back of the bench that bounds the upper square. This bench has been called one of the pieces most worthy of the highest esteem in all the history of design. Josep M. Jujol collaborated in the decoration.

He was one of Gaudís most brillaint disciples. The architectural genius also planned the interior streets in the park, the viaducts and the rustic stone porticos which connect the different ground levels. They are integrated in a natural way into the terrain, following the lines of mountain itself. Although it is difficult to make comparisons between the different works of Gaudí (since each of them is unique and fascinating), Park Güell is perhaps the one that was produced with the greatest expense of artistic energy.

Cervantes and Don Quijote in Barcelona

Legend has it that Cervantes stayed for a time in Barcelona, but when he was here was, until recently, unknown. Now a book has been published, by Martí de Riquer, well documented and full of details, that demonstrates that he was in Barcelona in 1610, when he was sixty two, a short time before Don Quijote and Sancho were to arrive.

The two heroes were supposed to have gone to Zaragoza, but when Quijote de Avellaneda appeared, Cervantes became irritated and sent the nobleman and his page to Barcelona. They arrived in the city on June 24, the feast day of San Juan, to meet the bandit Roque Guinarda. They had several exciting adventures, like the one of the talking head; their visit to the print shop of Sebastia Cormellas, in the Calle del Call; and a ship chase, until Don Juan was defeated on the beach of the Barceloneta and returned to his home town.

Then, in chapter 72, Cervantes praised Barcelona as he never did any other city: "Barcelona, archive of courtesy, resting place of foreigners, hospital of the poor, home of the brave, revenge of the offended and friendliness pleasingly returned, unique in its setting and its beauty".

Shortly afterwards, Don Quijote died, having fully recovered the use of his mind.

❖ La Barceloneta and the Parc de la Ciutadella★

The extensive Parc de la Ciutadella and the crowded neighbourhood of La Barceloneta share a past that, to a certain extent, binds them (although their development in the urban context has been divergent), as much as their geographic proximity. The opinion that a person in Barcelona might have had of the two areas two hundred years ago, for example, would have been the opposite of that of today's citizen. Two centuries ago the Ciutadella was a shameful barracks and La Barceloneta an appealing seamen's quarter full of one-storey houses. Today the barracks has become a park, and the quarter one of the most densely populated and most clearly deteriorated quarter of those of the city.

Once Felipe IV had dominated Barcelona, after his siege of 1714 and the abolition of the institutions proper to the city, such as the Consell de Cent, and proper to the kingdom, such as La Generalitat, he chose to make his power patently visible. One year later the monarch from Castille ordered a gigantic military fortress to be built in the eastern part of the walled area of the city. The terrain where the fortress was to be built was the site of part of the Ribera quarter. The houses there were torn down, more than a thousand of

In the popular Barceloneta, the city has finally re-encountered the sea and the beach, after having turned its back on them for so long.

them disappearing in less than three years time. The initial idea of building a neighbourhood on the beach outside of the walls was born of the necessity of providing homes for those of the Ribera who had been dispossessed. In fact, the same military engineer who designed the Ciutadella, the Frenchman Prosper de Verboom, also designed the new quarter in 1718. The present-day Barceloneta is from a later date though, as it was built in 1753. The latter project, which was carried out in its entirety, is the work of another military engineer, Juan Martín Carmeño. Thus, the past of La Barceloneta is linked with that of the Ciutadella. Their later development, however, followed lines of urban growth that were diametrically opposed.

La Barceloneta is located on land that was won from the sea by sedimentation processes. It is laid out in the shape of a triangle pointing into the sea. Two of its three sides, bordered by the Passeig Nacional and the Passeig Maritim, face the harbour and the beach of Barcelona. Both of the promenades are very popular with tourists, perhaps the greatest attraction of the quarter. The Passeig Nacional is dotted with locally popular restaurants, while the Passeig Maritim provides a long balcony open onto the Mediterranean. Nevertheless, for lovers of the different facets of the urban setting, the most interesting feature is surely the tangle of streets enclosed within the triangular space. They provide one of the most complete

Original greenhouse in the Parque de la Ciutadella.

examples maintained in Europe today of a Barroque urban area. The basic component of La Barceloneta is the elongate, very narrow city block. The idea was to have all the blocks of dwellings face onto two streets, and thus avoid the need for interior patios. In the beginning the houses were to have a ground and a first floor, and their façade was to be designed according to a single model.

During the xix century, this building code kept on growing in permissiveness, so that four-storey buildings were allowed to be put up, way out of proportion with the narrowness of their delimiting streets. This is perhaps why today's Barceloneta is no longer a picturesque seamen's community. It has become plagued by problems, stemming no doubt from the deterioration that

Antoni Tàpies was the creator of this extraordinary work found in the Parc de la Ciutadella, a homage to Pablo Picasso.

accompanies excessive population density.

The particular history of the Ciutadella is completely the opposite, as was mentioned. From its status of an enemy of the city, it has changed into the citizen-friendly one of city park, one of the few such that the city has. The military Ciutadella was laid out in the shape of a five-pointed star, with five more bastions, also pointed, that defended the straight stretches of its walls. Since 1869 it has belonged to the city. In its interior there are, on the one hand, the buildings that housed the military community, and on the other, the ones that were built for the Universal Exposition (1888). The former are found on both flanks of what was the parade ground, today made into French-style radiating gardens, with a pond in their centre presided over by a sculptural work by Josep Llimona entitled *Desconsol* (Affliction). On the eastern side there is what was once the arsenal, today the seat of the **Parlament de Catalunya** (II, C5), one of the politically most important institutions of the autonomous community, and the **Museu d'Art Modern** (II, C5), which contains works from the XVIII, XIX and beginnings of the XX centuries.

What was once the residence of the military government is still standing to the west of the parade grounds. Today it is used as a secondary school for the educating of a good number of students. The building was designed by Prosper de Verboom, likewise the author of the interesting military **church** beside the ex-residence.

The area built up in 1888 is that

which runs alongside the Passeig de Picasso. You can enter the area through the **Arc de Triomf** (I, B3), built by the architect Josep Vilaseca where the Passeig de Lluís Companys begins.

Besides the monumental Arch, the structure most representative of the Exposition that still remains is the one known as the "Castell dels Tres Dragons" (Castle of the Three Dragons), the work of the Modernist architect Lluís Domènech i Montaner, who designed it as a coffee shop-restaurant for the great event. Among the building's many different interesting aspects are: the use of unfaced brickwork (it was considered to be an inferior material at that time); the unified architectural volumes used; and the playful spirit that animates the decoration (whose historical tone was so much in vogue in that time). Once the Exposition was over, Domènech himself set up an applied arts workshop in which the best craftsmen of the Modernist movement worked. Today it is the seat of the **Museo de Zoología.**

Further along you encounter the **greenhouse** and the **Museo de Geología** (I, B-C3), both built for the Exposition in 1888.

The upper zone of the park is the site of an English type of garden; that is to say, it is crossed by sinuous paths; has a lake on which you can go for a row and a monumental cascade built by Josep Fontserè, on which a student of architecture collaborated, a fellow by the name of Gaudí. In the lower zone is the **Parque Zoológico de Barce-**

lona (the zoo), whose collection is headed by the only albino gorilla in the world, the famous "Copito de Nieve".

Outside the area of the park, on the Passeig de Picasso, there is an interesting sculpture in homage to the artist from Malaga, who spent some years in Barcelona before moving to Paris. The sculpture is the work of the Catalan Antoni Tàpies. The most surprising feature of the sculpture is the material from which it is composed, in no way related to the stone or metal normally used in this kind of thing; and its glass protective structure, over which water runs continuosly. A complicated device prevents the glass from getting fogged up. It

The aestheticly pleasing towers of the Parc de l'Espanya Industrial.

Dama i cell *is perhaps the most attractive motif in the Parc de l'Escorxador, an open space dedicated to the memory of Joan Miró.*

is perhaps a bit too exageratedly delicate, although this same fragility in the midst of its urban jungle setting certainly does make it even more attractive.

❖ Barcelona's Squares and Parks

The Ciutadella is the largest park within the city of Barcelona; another matter is the forested park in the Sierra de Collserola and the Botanic Park on Montjuïc. Not taking into account these last two parks, which are outside the city boundaries, you might reach the conclusion that green space is what the city most lacks. The city government's efforts to make squares and gardens of the little space that is available are certainly laudable. This patience-testing task has

begun to produce some visible results. Among the old city parks, and the ones built in the decade of the 1980's, there are some that are worth visiting. Some have been included in the description of the itineraries (Moll de la Fusta, Jardí de la Industria, Plaça del Sol); others are described below.

Parc de Joan Miró (II, D1), (between the Carrer Tarragona and Carrer Aragó), located in the terrain of the old municipal slaughterhouse, so that it is also known as the Parc de l'Escorxador. The space most characteristic of the park is an enormous open square presided over by a lovely sculpture by Joan Miró entitled *Dona i Ocell* (woman and bird).

Parc de l'Espanya Industrial (beside the railway station of

Sants-Barcelona Central), a space from the urban renewal project in the textile industries area. The park combines three perfectly integrated areas, which are the garden zone, a lake with irregular shoreline, and some showy towers that connect the different ground levels of the street and l'Espanya in an aesthetically pleasing way.

Across the street from the railway station is a square without plants, a "hard" square, as the towns-folk call it. It is the **Plaça dels Paisos Catalans,** with different pieces of urban furniture, such as fountains, benches and roofs, all exquisitely designed. The square is the work of the architects H. Piñon and A. Viaplana.

In others areas a little further away from the city centre similar results have been achieved by making old factories into modern parks. Such is the case of the **Parc de la Pegaso,** In the Sant Andreu del Palomar quarter, or in the very up-to-date **Parc de l'Estació del Nord.** In the crowded neighbourhood of **El Carmel** you find the **Parc de la Creueta del Coll,** which affords visitors a view of the magnificent sculptures of Eduardo Chillida.

❖ The Nou Barris

There is an old Barcelona, forged over the course of centuries within the restricted walled part, saturated with monumental buildings, its stones soaked in history. There is also a Barcelona that bet on the future, with its modern streets and buildings, while not forgetting the present, with its unique artistic features.

But time was not to be detained in the centuries of the Gothic, nor at the key dates of the grand expositions in 1888 and 1929. Barcelona has gained another face since then, an anonymous, functional, sometimes chaotic face, often times the face of speculation, completely lacking in anything memorable at all. Its only role was that of providing dwellings for the population of immigrants coming to Barcelona from everywhere in Spain, attracted by its economic boom. These new neighbourhoods were born mostly in the decades of the fifties and sixties, in the belt around the Eixample, to the north and east. The merger of eleven of these outlying quarters has produced the district known as Nou Barris (new neighbourhoods). The name was given to the zones most effected by the municipal planning of the beginnings of the seventies, an example of the penultimate Barcelona, the one whose origens were the darkest. The area that is today the site of these neighbourhoods (that are not always characterized by optimum living conditions) was an agricultural zone until the decade of the fifties. In 1952 the first group of apartment blocks were built in the heart of Verdum. They were called the Cases del Governador, made up of 900 flats with dining room, kitchen, bathroom and two bedrooms, none of them with a surface area larger than 25 square metres. Which is to say, they were match-box homes.

Until the middle of the eighties, Nou Barris could only offer urban

---

The Neighbourhoods

The geographical layout of Barcelona is relatively simple, due to the symmetry in its design. Next to the sea and in the middle is the Ciutat Vella, made up of the three zones of the old city, between La Rambla and the Via Laietana, whose centre was the Roman colony, and in which you find the palace of the government of Catalonia (Generalitat), and that of the city; to the right of the Ciudad Vella is the neighbourhood of La Ribera, the site of seamen's homes and textile factories, which provided the basis for the growth, culture and enrichment of the city and its Mediterranean empire; and to its left is El Raval, a workers' quarter and centre of exciting nightlife, which is bound in the future to have the highest density of cultural institutions. All of this zone, in which the city's history transpired until the XVII century, was enlarged in the XVIII century when the quarter of La Barceloneta was added, with its factories and seamen's homes.

The grand grid of the streets of Eixample encloses all this older zone. The grid was designed by Cerdà in the middle of the XIX century. Built up between 1870 and 1931, this central zone comprises the bourgeois quarter of the Dreta (right) del Eixample; the Distrito Central de Negocios (CBD) is there, and many Modernist buildings. It also comprises the Esquerra (left) del Eixample, middle and working-class, with its grand service institutions, such as the universtiy, the seminary, the fire department, the Hospital Clínico, the Universidad Industrial, and the prison Cárcel Modelo.

The neighbourhoods of factories and worker's homes spread around the Eixample to the right, with names like Poble Nou, Sant Martí de Provençals, Sant Andreu, and Horta. In the centre is the classic Gràcia, now the fiefdom of youth; and to the left, another zone of factories and workers' quarters in the middle class areas of Sants and Les Corts, along with the residences of the upper classes in Sant Gervasi, Sarrià and Pedralbes.

---

disasters of this type. But after that date the policy of improving the outlying districts has managed to awaken in these quarters an interest that is not always negative.

The star of the urban renewal of the outlying districts is the **Plaça de Llucmajor.** An imposing *Republica* has been erected there, the work of Viladormat. In the times of the Republic it presided over the intersection of Passeig de Gràcia and Avinguda Diagonal. A. Vilaplana and H. Piñon recently designed its sculp-

tural base. The monument is surprisingly visually effective, above all when you take into account the contrasting styles employed.

An interesting group of expresionist sculpture by J. Plensa and E. Pladevall has been set up in the **Plaça Francesc Layret,** off to one side of the Via Júlia. The buildings along the Via Júlia are also outstanding, as are too the Plaça de Sóller and the Avinguda de Rio de Janeiro, all of them ornamented with contemporary sculptural works.

There are two places worth visiting in the neighbouring quarter of Montbau, at the bottom of the Passeig de Vall d'Hebron. The first is the **Parc del Laberint,** a very well-maintained romantic garden in the centre of which is a labyrinth made up of hedges, full of inviting corners. The gardens that are planted round about the **Velodrom d'Horta** are also outstanding. They are dotted with a set of gigantic letters designed for the spot by the poet of the visual, Joan Brossa.

❖The Monasterio de Pedralbes★★

Although the **Monasterio de Santa María de Pedralbes** is located today within the bounds of the city, as a result of an inexorable urban sprawl, originally it was built for a cloistered community, far from the city of that time. The remains of its walls testify to that original function.

In fact, in among its buildings you find the houses of the monastery's many servants. There is even a small Franciscan convent, El Conventet, where the friars, who were in the service of the nuns, were lodged. The residential nature of the neighbourhood that grew up around the monastery has contributed to the preservation, to a certain extent, of the tranquility and peace that these stones exude. Inside, nuns belonging to a community from the order that has inhabited the place for seven hundred years continue with their rigorously cloistered lives. The monastery was founded in 1326 by Queen Elisenda de

The cloister of the Monastery of Santa María de Pedralbes, which dates from the XIV century, is an outstanding example of Catalan Gothic art.

Montcada, the fourth wife of Jaume II. One year and a half afterwards there were twelve nuns and fifteen novices living in it. Seven years later the number had grown to more than sixty.

The entrance to the place is on Carrer del Monestir that runs into the lovely square of the same name. To the right there is a staircase and to the left a way down that leads to the gates of the original walled area.

The monastery's prison occupied the tower by the upper gate. The side wall of a Gothic **church** gives onto the square where the belfry and the church doors are. The simplicity of the lines of the building is its greatest virtue.

The interior of the church is made up of a single spacious nave, divided into one part for public use and another for the cloistered nuns. Its walls were once adorned with precious jewels and old altars, but during the second half of the XIX century nonsensical reforms were carried out, financed by the sale of some of the decorative items. Robbers took care of the rest. Even after all of that, the funeral **monument** of Queen Elisenda is still wonderful. The queen died in 1364, and a splendid recumbent statue of hers was carved on top of her sarcophogus.

Next to the church is the wonderful **cloister,** straight out of the Catalan Gothic of the XIV century, the centre of monastic life in Pedralbes. Its square area has three floors on which are the rooms of the cloister. The chapter room, **Sala Capitular,** is especial-

ly fine. There is a Plateresque-style fountain in one of the corners of the cloister.

The chapel **Capilla de Sant Miquel,** one of the most unusual rooms of the monastery, is located between the church and the cloister. It once was the day cell of the Abess. The room is decorated with magnificent mural paintings, done by Ferrer Bassa in the year 1343.

❖ Tibidabo★

As was mentioned in the beginning of this itinerary, Barcelona uses a peculiar system of directions for its orientation. The massif of El Tibidabo (or the Sierra de Collserola) forms one pole of the system's sea-mountain axis. This mountain range is bounded by two rivers, the Besós and the Llobregat (which also bound the flatland), and is composed of a line of knolls and low mountains that reach maximum elevations of 200 to 530 m above sea level. The southeast face of the massif (which overlooks the city) is made up of an abrupt rise of 400 m, which makes Tibidabo look even higher from the streets of Barcelona, and also affords spectacular views of all of the city from the vantage point of its peak.

The name "Tibidabo" is taken from the scene on the mountain where Christ was tempted by the devil, who offered him all the wealth of the earth with the words "Omnia tibi dabo" (All of this I will give thee). In fact, this is not the only case of a biblical place name in the mountains. There is also a Hebrón valley, and

The amusement park on Tibidabo provides anyone who visits it with not only some fascinating rides, but also unique views of Barcelona.

Monte Carmelo. It seems that these places were given the names of places in Palestine by a community of hermits that lived on the slopes of the mountain in the XIV century.

When San Juan Bosco visited Barcelona in 1886, the lands of the summit of Tibidabo were offered to the Italian saint. The idea was that he should go about building an expiatory church dedicated to the Sacred Heart. That same year a small **hermitage** was erected, and in 1902 the cornerstone of the present-day church was laid. The original project was the work of Enric Sagnier, the favourite architect of the wealthy Catalan bourgeoisie. Its medieval air is accentuated by the wall around the Neogothic building, perhaps inspired by nostalgia for the city walls that had been demolished only a short time before. The work on the church was interrupted by the Civil War, and was not finished until nearly the end of the decade of the fifties.

Beside the church there is an amusement park open every day, the **Parque de Atracciones.** It has a magnificent **Museo de Autómatas.** Since 1901 a rack and pinion railway climbs up to the summit of Tibidabo from the streets of the city.

Another magnificent engineering work has been built for the 1992 Olympic Games; the **Communications Tower of Collserola** is a phenomenal needle, with a thirteen-storey main body that rises 268 m above its base on the summit.   ◆

EXCURSIONS FROM BARCELONA

Even though the monumentality and dynamism of the city is greatly appealing, a visit to Barcelona will still be incomplete if it does not include a tour through some of the truly unique spots to be found throughout the province. The excursions described herein also offer the counterpoint to the hubbub of the streets and the overpowering motorcar, the buildings, which dominate the cityscape. The three places which are described in these itineraries have exactly the opposite characteristics, in that they are places in which to relax in the solitude and beauty of nature.

You may also be surprised to see the massif of Montseny at such a short distance from Barcelona. Here stone draws magic pictures in the sky, and you will see landscapes as splendid as those of the daring heights of the peaks and astonishing thickness of the woods of Montseny. Finally, Sitges constitutes a perfect complement to the city, with its ambience, its streets and museums. It is also a great spot to enjoy nature from the seaside, the perpetual lover of Barcelona and of much of its province.

Excursion

1

❖ Montserrat

Although there is a road which goes right into the sanctuary of Montserrat, it is a better idea to leave your car in the Colonia Gomis, or else take the train, Ferrocarriles de la Generalitat, from the Plaça d'Espanya in Barcelona. You can then take the funicular and enjoy the delightful panoramic view while you cover the last leg of the journey. Montserrat is at a distance of some 35 km from Barcelona. From the north of the city you can take the A 18 motorway (Barcelona-Terrassa-Manresa), or from the south the A 7 motorway until you come to the exit for Martorell; from there you follow the signs to Montserrat.

Montserrat is appealing for many different reasons. After the waters that once covered Catalonia withdrew from the land, the action of wind, water and earthquakes on the massif's exposed geologic

Located on a mountain beyond description, the Monastery of Montserrat is much more than the spiritual and religious symbol of Catalonia.

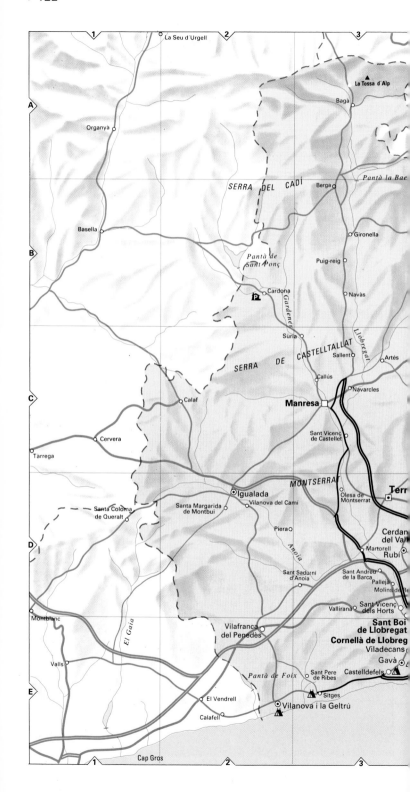

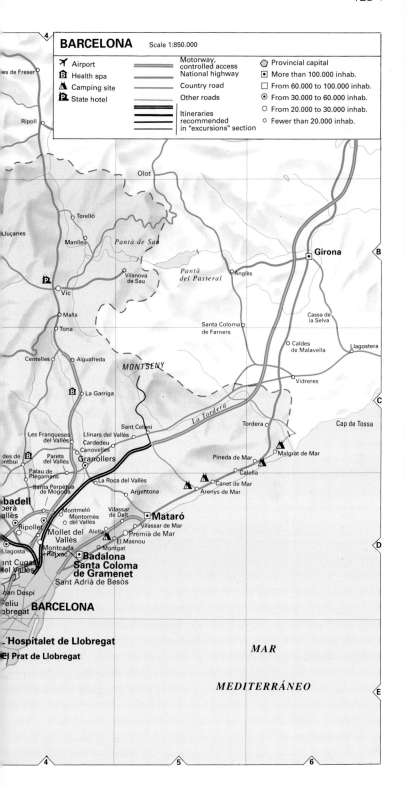

From the village of Montserrat, the massif seems to be located in a landscape dominated by the shapes of a magical geology.

materials (a sedimentary conglomerate, held together in a clay-limestone matrix from the Tertiary Period) eroded it into almost magical shapes and forms. Its highest point, the summit of Sant Jeroni, reaches a height of 1,325 m, while the monastery is built at a height of 723 m.

This imposing massif is 10 km long and 5 km wide, with a total perimetre of some 25 km. From the viewpoints set up on its summit, on clear days you can see practically all the territory of Catalonia. Its second great appeal stems from its rich symbolic significance, manifested in the devotion to the statue Mare de Deu de

Montserrat, an exquisitely beautiful Romanesque-style painted wood carving, whose colours have got darker and darker with the passing of the centuries, until the statue of the Virgen is today known by the popular sobriquet of La Moreneta (The Dark-skinned One). One particular historian of the sanctuary correctly described the statue as follows: "an elegant diadem crowns her head, a cushion is used to rest her feet on, finely shod. Her dress is composed of a tunic, cloak and cornet in the form of a net which falls gracefully from underneath her crown, halfway down her shoulders. In her right hand she holds a ball; her left hand rests lightly on the shoulder of the Christ Child, who is seated on her motherly lap, dressed in the same way as she except for the cornet, and is crowned as is the Virgen. His right hand is raised in blessing, his left holds a pine cone. The statue of the seated Virgen measures some 95 cm in height. Her body is small, in the style of the period, which lends the statue an air of firmness and spirituality, full of charm" (A. Albareda, 1931).

History and legend mix together round this dark Virgen. According to popular belief, this is the oldest existing statue of the Virgen. Supposedly it was carved from sittings of the Virgen herself, by Saint Luke. Saint Peter brought it along with him on one of his journeys to Barcelona, and left it in the catacombs which are today the site of the church Iglesia de San Justo y Pastor.

In the times of the Moorish invasion, out of fear that the carving might be destroyed, it was hidden in a cave in the nearby Sierra de Montserrat. There it stayed hidden during several centuries until some little shepherds from Monistrol saw a tremendous shining that came from the place on seven consecutive Saturdays. After the statue was discovered, the bishop in whose care it was placed wanted to return it to Barcelona. But while it was being taken there, those who carried it stopped to take a rest. When they started to go on, none of them, not even the strongest, was able to lift the statue from the ground. It seems that the Virgen had decided to stay in the mountains; in her honour a sanctuary was erected on the spot.

There are also several explanations for the colour of the Virgen's skin. Some people attribute her "tan" to the sunshine she was exposed to during the journeys she made with Saint Peter; others, to the smoke from a fire in the catacombs where the statue was kept.

History is much less explicit in its explanations, although there are documents that have survived from the IX century relating to the five hermitages that existed then on the mountain.

In the year 1025 the Abbot Oliva founded the Monasterio de Nuestra Señora de Montserrat, which was administered by the one in Ripoll. Montserrat finally became independent in the XV century. From the beginning it distinguished itself from the other Benedictine abbeys (which were dedicated mainly to intramural works) by attracting large numbers of pilgrims, who came to worship at the feet of the statue of the Virgen.

The original Romanesque hermitage was replaced by a church in the XVI century. A part of it is still standing. French troops destroyed the sanctuary in 1811, so that the greatest part of its architectural structures come from the period of its reconstruction in this century. Besides being a centre for the worship of the Virgen Mary, Montserrat has become a national symbol of Catalonia and the bulwark of its cultural heritage, as you will be able to see from its extensive library and paintings gallery.   ◆

Excursion

2

❖ Sitges

The motorway that goes from Barcelona towards the airport and Casteldefels leads to a winding highway that crosses through the Massif of El Garraf, a mountain chain bereft of vegetation, rough and troubling in appearance. The calcareous rock is broken abruptly by caves and caverns produced by the forces of erosion, and scarcely covered by a low growth of brush. This deserted landscape had been used as a rubbish dump for all kinds of refuse, but since 1986 it has been protected, made into a Parque Natural to prevent its further despoiling. For lovers of out-of-the-way places there is an information office in **Vallgrassa** (open from 10 h to 15 h). Its highest summits are La Morella (592 m) and El Rascler (572 m).

In the first break in the coastal cliffs, where there is a space betweeen them and the sea, you find **Sitges,** one of the most appealing towns in the Province of Barcelona. You can reach it by train as well as by highway.

The reasons for going to this coastal town include the crossing of the Massif of El Garraf,

The Palacio Maricel, headquarters of one of the three museums found in Sitges, is the neighbour of the Iglesia de Santa Tecla.

The quietest, most peaceful spot in Sitges is El Recó de la Calma, which is found between the Museu Cau Ferrat and the Palacio Maricel.

as well as the use in summer of the town's carefully-maintained beaches, its tree-shaded promenades, its welcoming squares and streets, and its unique night-time ambient.

Nevertheless, there are more reasons yet for visiting Sitges; the town's history is rich in literary and artistic associations, and has a notable cultural heritage. It also stages almost uninterrupted cultural performances and activities. Sitges has three museums that are interesting not only for their collections, but also for the splendid buildings in which they are housed, and for the lovely streets on which they are located.

Firstly there is the museum **Museu Cau Ferrat,** built on some rocks right on the coastline. This house was built in 1893 by F. Rogent on the site of a fisherman's house, and was the residence of the Modernist Catalan painter Rusiñol (1861-1931). He inspired the famous Fiestas Modernistas which were held at the

turn of the century in Sitges, and which attracted the best artists and intellectuals of the period. Besides having an impressive collection of Rusiñol's decorative

Gothic window with a panelled arch of the Maricel Museum.

Santiago Rusiñol

Of all of the people from Barcelona's history, the most popular and the one most talked-about was Santiago Rusiñol, a great leader of the Modernist movement and a centre of attention during his time. He was a very interesting person, whose characteristics are best expressed through contrasts: he was personally wealthy, but he preferred a bohemian life to that of the higher social classes; he was a painter, but enjoyed his greatest success as a writer; was born in Barcelona, but spent half his life in Paris, in Majorca, in Sitges and Aranjuez, where he died; He was Catalan, and even a Catalan nationalist, who wrote in Catalan, Castellano and in a hybrid language; he was a comic, but basically melancholic; married, but spent more time with his friends than with his wife; defended art for art's sake but, nevertheless, was satirical; and his best-known work is a novel, L'auca del senyor Esteve, *but it is better known in its theatre version, in which Barcelona is portrayed as a city whose soul is contained in the hearts of its shopkeepers, his fellow citizens.*

art, this museum houses a stunning painting collection, in which the paintings of Rusiñol stand out, along with those of his contemporaries, some of them of considerable historical value, such as the one signed jointly by Casas and Rusiñol, who are mutually depicted. There is also a lovely Picasso from 1901. Across the street is the **Palacio de Maricel,** which still has a few Gothic doors and windows, and an interesting museum inside. Between the two museums there is a tranquil little square, named El Racó de la Calma (the Corner of Calm).

At number one on the Calle San Gaudenci there is a house from the end of the XVIII century with perfectly intact furniture from the period, which has become the **Museu Romantic.** ◆

Excursion

3

❖ Montseny

The Sierra of Montseny is the highest pre-coastal massif south of the Pyreneés. Its summit of *El Turó de l'Home* reaches an altitude of 1,712 m, while there are another two peaks of similar height, *Les Agudes* (1,706 m) and *El Matagalls* (1,694 m). These peaks and the high plateau of La Calma (1,350 m) were incorporated in the *Parque Natural del Montseny* in 1977. The park has been declared a Reserve of the Biosphere by UNESCO.

The park is found to the north of the Province of Barcelona, on the border with the Province of Girona; the northern foothills of the Sierra fall within the Province of Girona, and are the site of an interesting group of communities, such as **Hostalric, Breda, Riells** and **Arbúcies.** From the city of Barcelona you can reach the area by car by taking the A 7 motorway for 32 km to the exit to **Sant Celoni**, which is almost the only way to do the itinerary through the Sierra.

A highway starts out from Sant Celoni, situated on the slopes of the Sierra, to go climbing up in the direction of **Santa Fe del Montseny** (21 km), a place where you will find an informa-

On the highest peak in the Montseny mountain range, El Turó del'Home, the vegetation takes on beautifully fantastic shapes.

tion office for the Parque Natural, as well as other services.

From this point you can choose from among several options, according to your tastes and the time you have available. The Sierra is enormous, and there is no lack of natural and historic points of interest. A good idea to begin with would be to get a stout staff and set off on a hike through the countryside. The stroll would be especially fine on summer days, since the sun hardly penetrates the deep shade cast by the foliage of the pines, holm oaks, chestnut trees, beech trees, and (in some parts) spruce trees.

During the XVI and XVII centuries, the dense forest was the location

Tower from ancient Catalonia's old Romanesque style.

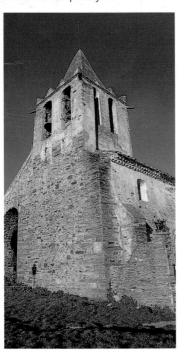

of the hideout of more than one band of thieves and highwaymen; some of them became as famous as Pere Roca Guinart, called *Perot lo Lladre,* who appeared as a character in Cervante's *Quijote,* or Joan Sala i Ferrer, the popular *Serrallonga,* native son of El Montseny.

Until the last century the wolf was the king of the fauna that lived in the Sierra. It has since then been exterminated, but the wild boar continues to survive there.

If you choose to make a hike you will certainly be happy to find one of the many sparkling springs that are born in the mountain chain. There is a forest path (with some stretches even paved) that leads to the summit of El Turó de l'Home, with panoramic views from the heights sure to please the lover of the great outdoors. The path begins at a point 7 km before you reach Santa Fe, and is clearly sign-posted.

Another possibility would be to complete the itinerary which begins and ends in Sant Celoni by car through the area of El Montseny, stopping to visit the most interesting places. A tour of this type involves about 100 km of driving; along the way you will find many places where you can stop to rebuild your strength with dishes from traditional Catalan cooking.

El Montseny also offers a wealth of lovely mountain landscapes which can be seen from the highway, and which you will go along discovering as you complete the tour of the massif.

Taking the highway out of **Sant Celoni,** and before you reach

Enchanting villages born in the shade of somber Romanesque-style churches are scattered throughout the mountain range of Montseny.

Santa Fe, you will pass near two little villages on the mountain slopes, called **Campins** and **Fogars de Montclús,** typical mountain communities built up around their Romanesque-style churches. At a distance of 14 km from Sant Celoni and a few metres after you have passed on your left the forestry service road to Turó de l'Home, there is a fine example of the vernacular architecture of Catalonia, in the form of a "masía" (country manorhouse) at the foot of the road. These structures are characterized by their central door, a semicircular arch with stone voussoirs, which are not covered, and a window above, also framed by stone. The ground plan is in the form of a rectangle and the roof is always peaked, with two slopes. These huge country estate houses include various outbuildings, such as stables, barns, porches and others whose disposition can vary greatly according to the nature of the work carried out in them, be it farming at the lower altitudes, or ranching at the higher ones.

Past Santa Fe, 7 km further on you will see the Romanesque hermitage **Ermita de Sant Marçal,** at an altitude of 1,107 m. It was consecrated in the XI century.

From Sant Marçal you will descend towards **Viladrau,** on the northern face of the massif, and following a route through **Seva** and **El Brull** ascend again in the direction of the pass Collado de Collformic.

The highway continues on towards **Sant Bernat** and the village of **Montsey,** places of undeniable charm, which are also well worth visiting. ◆

What to do
gastronomy, festivities, leisure and museums

*Guillermina Botalla (gastronomy). Juan Rosás (museums)
and ANAYA/touring team.*

On the following pages you will find information about the food, calendar of festivities, places in which to relax, museums; as well as a list of hotels and campgrounds, mountain refuges, and the addresses of such offices as those of the post, telegraph, telephone, mass media, tourist offices and transport companies.

The groups known as Los Castellers are the continuers of a living tradition in the fiesta of Barcelona, and a reflection of the strength and unity of these people. Above these lines, the oldest restaurant in the city, "7 Portes".

Gastronomy

Some writers maintain that Barcelona lacks its own particular style of cooking. If true, it is due to the fact that the city has absorbed customs and ingredients from all over Catalonia, which are very different, the ones from the others, because of the area's great geographic diversity. The interior has produced simple, unadorned dishes, while from the mountainous areas come solid stews; the southern coast gives us light aromatic dishes, while those of the Ampurdan do not hesitate to combine lobster, chicken and chocolate in the same casserole. Other factors include the influence throughout history of neighbouring countries, the effects of the much more recent fever, the nouvelle cuisine, and also the latest culinary experiments.

You will find all of this served up in the restaurants, but of course it is also available to the residents, either through recipes followed in home kitchens, or in the bare-essentials form of frozen and pre-cooked packaged meals, marketed with today's busy housewives as the target consumer. In the colourful Mercado de la Boquería, one of the lovliest markets in the world, you will find a gigantic and spectacular display of all the available produce in the city. One can learn more by taking a stroll through it, sniffing, looking, observing and listening, than by reading any printed text.

Home cooking

Through all the ups and downs of their city's history, the people of Barcelona have never overcome their weakness for European-style cooking. What has been called bourgeoise cooking in Barcelona is the result of a fortunate combination of the features of French, Italian and Catalan culinary arts. Many of the older dishes have been forgotten; others stubbornly survive. Such is the case of the festive dish of canneloni, a Sunday dinner dish par excellence, which in some households reaches a state of rare perfection by slightly modifying the Italian recipe. The tables of Barcelona also appropriated the macaroni, which is usually served with an addition of meat au gratin. It thus has come to form part of the most deeply loved dishes of many people in the city. There used to be an endless variety of dishes based on eggs, when they were still considered to be "good food", before the advent of the factory egg and the cholesterol syndrome. And there are the dishes based on the much-used rice, such as the "arroz a la Milanesa" (but a naturalized citizen of Barcelona) with fish, with rabbit. Lamb (native to these lands) was for some years considered to be inferior to veal, as used in the traditional *fricandó*, another cornerstone of home cooking. Curiously, this dish is not featured on the menus of the majority of restaurants, even those that specialize in this type of home cooking. The dish is a stew with a thick gravy, which is usually dotted with *moixernons.* And there is lots of pork, in the form of sausage and cuts of meat which were served as the normal aperitifs for the family meal; in the dish *cap i pota* (head and hooves), an astoundingly thick stew; pig's knuckles, served in a thousand ways, and pig jowls and roast sirloin. The pig is served in all its parts and in all its forms, with the only exception being the suckling pig, which is unkown in these parts.

Fitting in with the total absence of ostentation so typical of the Catalans, the daily meals of the middle and upper-middle classes were simple, modest soups, potato dishes, noodle casseroles, pork stews, greens and vegetables. Left-overs were eaten religiously, appearing in the delicious croquettes or "vieira" conches filled and served au gratin with a mixture of left-over roasts or fish and béchamel sauce.

From among the fishes, the cod is one of the favourites. It was especially so when its price made it affordable for even those whose budgets were restricted; it still is popular, despite the rise in price that has removed it from the category of the reasonably-priced. Housewives did wonderful things with the codfish; their principal miracle was the dish called *bacalla a la llauna* (codfish a la "tin"), named for the material of the casserole commonly used to prepare it in. The recipe for the dish was extremely simple, very typical of Barcelona and a cornerstone of the Catalan cuisine. But generally speaking, every kind of fish appears frequently on the tables here; if a preference does exist, then perhaps it is for the "rape" (anglerfish), one of the favourites. Finally, at the end of this section, there is space for an original dish from Barcelona called the "zarzuela", which is made from a great variety of fish and shellfish in a sauce of fried tomatoe and onion. It is a Barroque-style splurge of a dish, in which one can see evidence of the urge of the people to make sure that "nothing is lacking", something which runs counter to the supposed frugality of the Catalans.

Traditional cooking

On any list of dishes or foods considered to be typical of Catalonia, probably the first would have to be the "butifarra con judías blancas" (type of sausage with white beans) found so commonly in all the neighbourhood eating places. The secret in acheiving a greater or lesser degree of succulence lies in both the quality of the "butifarra" used, and the way that the previously boiled beans are fried.

One must also make mention of the *escudella i carn*

d'olla, the "cocido" (winter stew) in Catalonia that uses butifarra in place of the "chorizo" (red pepper sausage) of Madrid. Two types of butifarra are used, the "white" one and the "black", made with blood. In the orthodox *escudella* there must also be a giant meatball condimented with garlic and parsley. If one were going to talk about the most popular dish in Catalonia, one would have to speak of this *escudella* (which is the broth) and its *carn d'olla*.

Everyone in Barcelona likes this "stew" so much that, even though it was eaten every day during a period of some decades (or at least once a week), it had to be included on the menu of courses served at the family dinner table on Christmas day, at the meal which is considered the most important of the year. On the occasion of Christmas, the broth is thickened with the gigantic pasta called *galets* (elbows), and the huge meatball is usually replaced by tiny ones swimming in the broth.

The topic of Christmas ritual brings us to the subject of the roast turkey or capon, eaten here as it is in many other countries, but with the special touch of a stuffing made of pork sausage, dried apricots, prunes, pine nuts, truffles and chestnuts. The mixture of sweet and salty ingredients, along with the use of lard and cinnamon for roasts, is an old feature of Catalan cooking. While the use of lard from the pig is practically forbidden today due to its cholesterol content, it used to be fundamental to the preparation of roasts and many other dishes.

Catalonia is one of the few areas in Spain that celebrates the feast day of San Easteban, not so much because of any great devotion inspired by the saint, but because of its date, December 26. Those who have overindulged on Christmas day are thus free to stay home the following day and sleep or work off the excess, rather than have to go in to the office. True, some do say that in fact the motivation for the extra day off work is none other than the greedy desire to clean up the tasty leftovers from the previous day's feast.

Whatever the reason for the day's celebration, traditionally the dinner menu on the day after Christmas must include canneloni, to use up the roast that was not finished the day before. It must also include a strange dish called *arros de colls i punys* (rice with necks and feet) which makes use of those parts of the bird served the day before. Of course, according to the means of each family, overflowing dishes of lobster or some other kind of succulent treat are also served before these two above-mentioned dishes.

The calendar of Treats

Although the original celebrations for which certain dishes were prepared have changed, the dishes themselves are still prepared and consumed as of old.

This writer, is completely attached to certain culinary traditions, in spite of recent changes, and determined to maintain the customary consumption of ritual dishes on certain dates. These dates today may or may not coincide with the original feast day that was once then celebrated; for example, on "Lard Thursday" the pastry shops sell every imaginable kind of "coca" (Catalan variety of the pizza) topped with pig's crackling. The same thing occurs in the meat shops where they sell butifarra with egg, which is a white, pre-cooked butifarra which only on this occasion is sold with egg added. A kind of Spanish omelette is prepared with it.

But the section of sweets is especially delicious and varied. There is the "crema" for the feast day of San José (Catalan cream with carmelized sugar), which is now available all year round. During Lent, in Barcelona alone they consume tonnes of "buñuelos de viento" and "buñuelos de Emporda" (sweetrolls; the latter are drier and more substantial). At Easter time you have the "monas", sweet chocolate structures, the product of the efforts of Barcelona's pastry chefs, who are rather talented.

The Verbenas de San Juan and San Pedro (outdoor dancing) could not be held without the "coca", made with a flattened dough, generally decorated with sugared fruit and pine nuts, and washed down with generous draughts of "cava" (champagne-method wine). All Saints Day is the occasion for eating *panellets,* a sweet of different colours and tastes. The traditional "turrón" (nougat) is served for dessert at Christmastime, along with the crunchy "barquillos" (rolled wafer).

Mushrooms and bread with tomatoe

A stranger to Barcelona who happened to be walking through the woods and mountains near the city on a Sunday in the autumn would certainly find it perplexing to see a crowd of people walking along, bent over, looking at the ground. Men, women, children of all ages and conditions go armed with staffs, baskets and knives, all participating in the search for "setas" (mushrooms), the favourite sport in Catalonia. It does not matter that the tremendous competition makes the finding more difficult, or that at the end of the day's search the greater part of the harvest has to be thrown away because no one in the group is willing to take the responsibility for guaranteeing the edibility of some of the collection. Everyone is satisfied as long as the booty includes a certain number of *rovellons* (a variety of mushroom also known as "niscalo"). The people of Barcelona are really fond of this mushroom, which can appear in a dish as simple as that of "niscalos" with garlic and parsley. They are also delicious served with meat and accompanying the butifarra.

In any case, the variety of mushrooms eaten has been considerably increased in recent years. The city-dwellers have become epicures in the field of mushrooms, and their favourite restaurants have demoted their dishes of *rovelló* from its previous first place position to a lower ranking, replaced by dishes such as *ous de reig, surenys, ceps, rossinyols, llenegues, múrules, trompetes dels morts* (fungus and mushrooms all, the last with the evocative name "trumpets of death"), all of them now enjoying a period of popularity.

And what can be said of bread with tomatoe? It has been a constant feature of the Catalan diet for ages, for those of all social classes and circumstances, the object of real addiction and cause of genuine frustration. The frustration arises from the insistance of the Catalans in explaining to waiters and cooks how to go about preparing their basic sustenance, wherever in the world they may find themselves. Naturally, the hungry Catalan in a strange land is usually disappointed with the bread and tomatoe that he is served.

Really there is only one way to obtain perfect results in its preparation. One must use good "pan de payes" (the local bread, in large size called "hogaza"), ripe tomatoes, skillfully rubbed on the slices, first-class olive oil and salt. Any substitution of other ingredients in the recipe (such as the use of canned tomatoes) ruins the result.

The wines of Barcelona

There are eight D.O.'s (Denominación de Origen) in Catalonia: there is the Alella, with its famous white wines; the Emporda-Costa Brava, with their vineyards situated more to the north, from which outstanding reds and rosés are elaborated, along with the old, sweet "garnatxas"; the Conca de Barbera, with mostly whites and rosés; Costa del Segre, with its whites, reds, rosés and cavas; Penedes, a region in which the reds are beginning to achieve a prestige to rival that of the whites; Priorato, which produces mainly red and sweet wines; Tarragona, with its clarets, rosés, whites and reds; and finally, Terra Alta, with its potent reds and dry whites.

Wines elaborated from foreign grapes are more fashionable today, so that the Cabernet, the Chardonnay and the Merlot grapes are generally used for the highest-priced wines, but the offer is as diverse as are the tastes of the buying public, so that other varieties of grapes are also used.

The subject of Cava is something special in Catalonia, where it is considered to be the drink of drinks. It has become almost an obsession in Catalonia, justifiably so, considering its high quality.

There can be no fiesta here without bottles of the bubbly stuff, and as it is an ideal drink for any time of day or night, it is also becoming common to drink it by the glass in establishments called "champañerías" that specialize in serving this champagne-method sparkling wine. Likewise, it is frequently drunk with every course of the meal.

The experts in the field prefer the *brut* type in number of bottles sold. This type of Cava never contains more than 15 grammes of sugar per litre. Nevertheless, the *champagne* of France is still consumed in increasingly large quantities. While in the old days the respectable and well-off upper crust of Barcelona drank French champagne in the privacy of their own homes, so as not to put on a show of their opulence, their grandchildren do not hesitate to enjoy themselves drinking it in public. For the rest of the population, it continues to be only something spoken about, although its scarcity does not cause traumas among them. According to those who should know, Cava is the better drink.

Restaurants

The restaurants cited here are among the most traditional ones, or for some other reason are considered to be among the best. Of course the selection in this area here is quite incomplete; likewise not many restaurants featuring foreign cooking are included either, although there certainly are some interesting ones in the city.

Cassic Restaurants

Reno
Tuset, 27; tel. 200 91 29. Closed on Saturday during the summer. Justifiably called "Barcelona's classic". A great kitchen, with corresponding service and premises. Very good wine cellar. Average price from 7,000 to 8,000 pta.

Vía Veneto
Ganduxer, 10-12 (les Corts); tel. 200 70 24. Closed at lunchtime Saturday and Sunday. Luxurious, elegant, wisely combines fine cuisine with traditional dishes. Politicians and businessmen reserve its tables. Average price from 7,000 to 8,000 pta.

Modern Cooking

Azulete
Via Agusta, 281; tel. 205 59 45. Closed at lunchtime Saturday and Sunday. Marked Mediterranean influence in the cooking, without going to extremes. Menu featuring selection of traditional dishes. Beautiful premises. Average price between 7,000 and 7,500 pta.

Florian

Bertran i Serra, 20; tel. 212 46 27. Closed Sunday. Its cooking features mushroom dishes, bull-fighting dishes and Italian inspired ones, but Rosa Grau is a restless cook, always learning something, so that novelties are never lacking. Good wine and liqueur list; details are carefully taken care of. Average price from 4,000 to 5,000 pta.

Jaume de Provença

Provença, 88; tel. 230 00 29. Closed Sunday night and Monday. A solid establishment with an equally solid Catalan-inspired kitchen. Average price from 5,000 to 6,000 pta.

Neichel

Avinguda de Pedralbes, 16 bis; tel. 203 84 08. Closed Sunday.
Jean-Louis Neichel, from Alsace, has occupied the position of Cátedra of Chefs with his fine quality modern French cooking. Its desserts are also impressive, along with its wines and liqueurs. Average price from 6,000 to 7,000 pta.

Nostromo

Ripoll, 16; tel. 412 24 55. Closed Sunday. A café-book-store-restaurant, located in a basement loaded with history, where the imagination of Quim Marqués, the young chef, reigns over dishes which include the essence of Catalan cooking. Average price from 4,000 to 5,000 pta.

Odisea

Copons, 7; tel. 302 36 92. Closed Saturday at lunchtime and on Sunday. Pretty, refined and different, due to the personal-style cooking of Antonio Ferrer. Good wine cellar in keeping with the premises. Average price from 6,000 to 7,000 pta.

Catalan Cooking

Agustí

Vergara, 5; tel. 301 97 45. A few metres away from the Plaza de Cataluña, its cooking has always been Catalan-style, absolutely guaranteed to please. Average price from 2,000 to 3,000 pta.

Agut

Gignas, 16; tel. 315 17 09.
Closed Sunday night and Monday.
It has been in business for about 70 years, and has come to form part of the history of a dynasty of restaurant owners and operators. Average price from 2,000 to 3,000 pta.

Casa Isidro
Carrer de les Flors, 12; tel. 241 11 39. Closed Sunday, holidays and Saturday night during summer. One of the most famous, cleverest kitchens in Barcelona; Catalan cooking, French influence. Impeccable care with the details. Average price from 2,000 to 3,000 pta.

Casa Leopoldo
Sant Rafael, 24; tel. 241 30 14. Closed Sunday night and Monday. Traditional, having been in business for more than 60 years; famous for its fish dishes and for the quality of the ingredients used. Average price from 2,000 to 3,000 pta.

Culleretes
Quintana, 5; tel. 317 30 22. Closed Sunday night and Monday. This could be considered the oldest restaurant in Barcelona, 200 years old, counting the period of time when it functioned as a "chocolatería". Its character, its interior, its cooking, home-style in the best sense of the term, are all intact. History hangs from its walls, immortalized in an impressive collection of photographs of the people who have sat at its tables. Average price from 2,000 to 3,000 pta.

Chicoa
Aribau, 71; tel. 453 11 23. Closed Saturday night and Sunday. Its codfish dishes have won it fame, but it offers other fine options. Average price from 4,000 to 5,000 pta.

Egipto
Jerusalén, 3; tel. 317 71 80. Closed Sunday. Its reasonable prices are not its only attraction, as it also uses fresh ingredients from the nearby Mercado de la Boquería. Average price from 2,000 to 3,000 pta.

Eldorado Petit
Dolores Monserdà, 5; tel. 204 51 53. Closed Sunday. Emporda-style cooking from Sant Feliu de Guíxols featured in this establishment, set up in a pretty house in the quarter Barrio de Sarrià. Average price from 5,000 to 6,000 pta.

Envalira
Planeta, 10 (Plaça del Sol); tel. 218 58 13. Closed Sunday night and Monday. Informal, busy and always crowded. Very renowned Arroz a la Milanesa (rice dish), while the rest of its menu is also interesting. Average price 2,500 to 3,000 pta.

Gargantua i Pantagruel

Aragó, 214; tel. 453 20 20. Closed Sunday. A place to get to know the wealth of the cooking of Lérida, although its menu is not limited to snails. Average price from 3,000 to 4,000 pta.

La Masía del Tibidabo

Plaça del Tibidabo,1; tel. 417 63 50. Closed Sunday night and Mondays if not a holiday. Panoramic views. Highly agreeable decoration and cooking which is an adequate introduction to the possibilities in Barcelona. Average price from 3,500 to 4,000 pta.

Roig Robí

Séneca, 20; tel. 218 92 22. Closed Sunday. Agreeable restaurant, with a good selection of the bourgeoise cooking of Barcelona on its menu. Average price from 4,000 to 5,000 pta.

Senyor Parellada

Platería, 37; tel. 315 40 10. Closed Sunday. Its spirit, treatment of its clients and cooking are those of an excellent Catalan boardinghouse. Very typical dishes, prepared by sure hands. Average price from 3,000 to 3,500 pta.

Siete Puertas

Passeig Isabel II, 14; tel. 319 30 33. This is the dean of such establishments in Barcelona. A must, pleasing, and never closed, with 24-hour service every day of the week. Catalan cooking on pretty, historic premises where everybody in the world has eaten. Average price from 3,500 to 4,000 pta.

Fish Dishes

Blau Marí

Moll de la Fusta, Edículo no. 2; tel. 310 10 15. Closed Monday. Designed like a snack bar on the waterfront in the harbour. Agreeable terrace, crowded at night in summer. Seafood dishes, different *bullabesas* and an ample variety of "tapas". Average price from 3,000 to 4,000 pta.

Can Majó

Almirante Aixada, 23; tel. 310 14 55. Closed Sunday night and Monday. In this establishment located in the Barceloneta they feature fish and rice dishes. Average price from 4,000 to 5,000 pta.

Peixerot

Tarragona, 77 (ground floor of Torres de Cataluña); tel. 424 69 69. Closed Sunday night. It is the younger brother, but not in terms of its merit, of one of the best restaurants specialized in seafood on the coast of Catalonia. Freshest of seafood ingredients. Average price from 4,000 to 5,000 pta.

Restaurantes del Real Club Marítimo
Muelle de España; tel. 315 02 56. Closed Sunday night and Monday. Well lit, very agreeable, hovering over the small craft in the pleasure craft harbour. Extreme care with details, such as the menu of coffees and teas, and the splendid oil that fills their oil cruets. Average price from 4,000 to 5,000 pta.

Some "Foreign-Food" Restaurants

Amaya
Ramblas, 20-24; tel. 302 10 37. Traditional and popular. Its menu offers a larger number of dishes typical of the Basque country. Cider and *txacolí* (white wine from the Basque country). Average price from 3,500 to 4,000 pta.

Botafumerio
Mayor de Gràcia, 81; tel. 218 42 30. Closed Sunday night and Monday. Great variety of shellfish and fish dishes typical of Galicia. Very attractive alternative of dining at the bar on tapas. Open from 13 h to 1 h. Average price from 6,000 to 7,000 pta.

Carballeira
Reina Cristina, 3; tel. 310 10 06. Closed Sunday, holiday nights and Mondays. Neither the quiet, nor silence, nor ceremonious manners are needed in this popular and always crowded Galician seafood restaurant. Average price from 3,000 to 4,000 pta.

Gorria
Diputació, 421; tel. 323 78 57. Closed Sunday and holiday nights. One of the best Basque-Navarra kitchens in the city, dishes made from the best ingredients. Average price from 4,000 to 5,000 pta.

In the area around Barcelona

Aranys del Mar
Hispania
Carretera Real, 54; tel. 791 04 57. Closed Sunday night and Tuesday. One of the best in Catalonia by the labours of the Rexach brothers, who know and use only the best ingredients in their unequalled manner. Exquisite service and lovely setting. Average price from 4,000 to 5,000 pta.

Badalona
Palmira
L'Escala, 2 (Barrio de Canyet); tel. 395 12 62. Open all year round. Very good kitchen, which does not ever

compromise on the quality of the ingredients used. Typical Barcelona dishes, some of them disappeared from the menus of other establishments. It has an agreeable garden. Average price from 3,000 to 4,000 pta.

Esplugues de Llobregat
Casa Quirse
Laureano Miró, 202; tel. 371 10 84.
Closed Sunday night, Monday and holidays. French influence in quality Catalan cooking in an old inn where the stage coaches used to stop. During the hunting season, serves a variety of game dishes. Average price from 4,000 to 5,000 pta.

Granollers
Fonda Europea
Anselm Clavé, 1; tel. 870 03 12. Family atmosphere, agreeable, model sample of traditional Catalan cooking. Average price from 2,000 to 3,000 pta.

Sant Celoní
Racó de Can Fabes
Sant Joan, 6; tel. 867 28 51. A gastronomer's Mecca, in spite of the youth of the restaurant and its owner. His kitchen is creative while being unmistakably linked to the immediate surroundings of the Sierra de Montseny and the nearby coast. Average price from 4,000 to 5,000 pta.

Sant Pere de Ribes
Gran Casino de Barcelona
Finca Mas Soler; tel. 893 36 66. Open from 21 h to 1.30 h. Very near Sitges, a restaurant and casino that fit in with the sumptuous setting of an old nobleman's mansion. Good cellar. Average price from 5,000 to 6,000 pta.

Sant Sadurni d'Anoia
Mirador de las Caves
Carretera Ordal, km 4.5; tel. 899 31 78.
From its windows one can see the endless expanse of Penedes' vineyards. Frequented by lovers of Cava; they serve Catalan specialities. Average price from 3,000 to 4,000 pta.

Vilanova i la Geltrú
Peixerot
Passeig Marítim, 56; tel. 815 06 25. Closed Sunday night during the winter. One of the great, authentic institutions of fish cusine. Seafood specialities elaborated with skill and using the best ingredients. Average price from 3,000 to 5,000 pta.

Museums

Fundació Joan Miró. Passeig de Miramar, Parque de Montjuïc. Tel. 329 19 08. Open Tuesday through Saturday from 11 h to 19 h. Thursday until 21.30 h. Closed Monday when not a holiday. The Foundation was set up by the painter Joan Miró as a centre of studies of contemporary art. It also exhibits a wide sample of the work of its founder. The building is the work of the painter's friend, J. L. Sert. It combines the modern with the architectural characteristics typical of the Mediterranean. A visit to the museum begins in the temporary exposition halls, where normally works by contemporary artists are displayed. The lighting system in these exhibition halls is especially interesting. The permanent exposition of the work of Miró begins with some panels which display the chronological development of the artist's work. The most outstanding of the tour through this part of the museum is the large *Tapis de la Fudació,* the early works exhibited in the Joan Prats salon, and the lithographs from the *Barcelona* series. These works are linked with those of the Pilar Juncosa gallery on the upper floor. You can go out on the terrace, where there is an open-air exposition of the sculpture of Miró. There is also an extensive collection of drawings. In the last gallery are works by the most important contemporary artists, donated in homage to Miró.

Museo Arqueológico de Cataluña. Passeig de Santa Madrona. Parque de Montjuïc. Tel. 423 21 49. Open from 9.30 h to 13 h and from 16 h to 19 h. Sunday and holidays from 10 h to 14 h. Closed Monday. The itinerary is chronological. One begins with remains from the Paleolithic in Catalonia, and goes on to the Neolithic and Eneolithic. The "cardial" and "campaniforme" pottery collection is outstanding. The Argárica culture comes next, with its corresponding pottery and the major find of the funeral dress and furnishings from Montilla. Next comes the evolution from the Bronze to the Iron Age, from the XII to the II century BC. in this section the metal objects from La Meseta and the Castillian funeral urns are the most outstanding. The rooms dedicated to the culture of the Balearic Islands (Majorca, Ibiza, Menorca, etc.) are especially interesting, with a period of evolution of 2000 years. You can see the Talyótic bronzes and the terracotta from Ibiza, of Punic inspiration. In the hallway that goes around the central area of the museum is an explanatioon of the world of Iberia, with some extraordinary pieces, such as the treasure from Tivissa.
In the central hexagon you find the most important objects in the museum's collection, such as the Escu-

lapio de Empúries (III century BC). The rest of the museum is dedicated to Roman archaeology, their circus mosaics, Greek and Roman material from Empúries, an extraordinary collection of glass and bronze objects, as well as sculptures. The tour ends with an exposition of Visigoth objects, among which are some outstanding pieces of jewelry.

Museo de Arte de Cataluña. Palau Nacional. Palau de Montjuïc. Closed to the public in 1991. Its collection includes the best works of Catalan art, and one of the best Romanesque art collections in Europe.

The tour begins with a display of Pre-Romanesque art, but the most interesting section in the museum is the extraordinary series of mural paintings, from the XII century in the Catalan Pyreneés. The style of the absidioles of Peret are wonderful. In the apse of Burgal is the portrait of the Countess who donated the paintings. The *graffitti* from the Bohí portico is something curious to see.

The two most imposing pieces are the groups from Santa María and Sant Clement de Taüll, from the XII century, and especially the Pantocrátor de Sant Climent (figure of Christ). The two groups are complimented by corresponding Romanesque furnishings.

From the Romanesque sculpture, the *Majestat Batlló,* a few Virgens and Descents are interesting. A few capitals are also interesting, such as that of the *Sacrificio de Isaac.* you can also see the major collection of Romanesque façades.

Next comes the painting from the transition from the Romanesque to the Gothic, such as the panels from Soriguerola, those from Vallbona, and a few altarpieces. There is an imposing baldachine by Tavernoles; from this period also are the Castillian paintings by Mahamud (Burgos). The museum's collection of Gothic art is important, too, since this period coincided with the domination of the Mediterranean by the Catalan-Aragones Crown. From the Gothic, with Italian influence, there are the very special paintings by the Serra brothers, such as their altarpiece from Sixena (from around the year 1360), and the Virgen with Christ Child between angel-musicians by Tortosa. Among the sculptures from this period are the outstanding pieces by Cascalls and the recumbent statue of one of the abads of Sant Cugat del Vallès. At the end of the XIV century the Catalan Gothic began absorbing more than strictly Italian influences, and entered a period of the "international" Gothic. The best from this period are the works by Lluís Borrassa and Bernat Martorell, and some panels from Aragón and Valencia. The sculptures of San Antonio de la Figura and the virgen de Sallent are especially beautiful. Flemish realism is embodied in the lovely panel of *Verge dels Consellers,* the work of Lluis Dalmau around the year 1444, where the five municipal magistrates of Barcelona are portrayed. But the best works from this period are those of Jaume Huguet; there is large collection of panels by him. Then too there are the works of his disciples, and some sculptures; and then comes the Renaissance, with paintings by Anye Bru, Joan Gasco and Pere Nunyes. The Barroque collections are less interesting, but include some acceptable artists, such as Juncosa, Tramulles and Montanya. The best from among them is Antoni Viladomat. The Barroque collection is completed with works by painters who were not Catalan, like Velázquez, El Greco, and others.

Museo de Arte Moderno. Plaça de les Armes. Parque de la Ciutadella. Tel. 319 57 28. Open from 9 h to 19.30 h. On Sunday only until 14 h. On Monday only after 15 h. It is the continuation of the Museo de Arte de Cataluña, and forms part of the same institution. It shares the building (which is the old arsenal of the fortress that Felipe V had built) with the Parlament de Cataluña. The museum has a collection with a wide selection of artists from the period which was fundamental to the art of Catalonia, the xix and xx centuries. The Neoclassic and Romantic works from the first half of the xix century are not on display. The tour begins with the works of Fortuny, the best being *La Vicaria* (1870) and *La batalla de Tetuán* (1863). Next to him are the realists Caba, Mercadé and Simó Gómez. Then come the works of Martí Alsina, who established the foundations of modern Catalan painting, and those of his disciple Joaquim Vayreda, who headed the School of Olot. The next paintings are by the formal realist Masriera *(invierno de 1882)* which depict the melancholic landscapes of Urgell. Of the sculptors' work, that of Agapito Vallmitjana is perhaps the best, along with the *Torero herido* by Rossend Nobas. Next comes the Modernist section, with some of the most important paintings from that movement being displayed. Outstanding are the works of Casas, Rusiñol and Utrillo, and the sculptures by Llimona. An impressive collection of Modernist objects and furniture follows, and then comes the painting of Francesc Gimeno, Sorolla, Regoyos, and others. Again there is more Catalan painting, this time by Canals and María Pidelaserra, followed by the Postmodernist work of Nonell (his best are the "gitanas") and Mir. A good selection of important works from the *noucentisme* movement follow, of a classic Mediterranean inspiration, and influenced by the other movements of the day; it was the movement that developed from Modernism in Catalonia.

From among the sculptors perhaps the most interesting are Manolo Hugué and Rebull, and from among the painters, Sunyer and Torres García; in a second phase, there were the sculptors Casanovas and Clara, and the painters Francesc Domingo and Josep de Togores. The sculpture of Gargallo and Juli González take you to the Vanguardist tendencies, the final section of the museum.

Museo Frederic Mares. Plaça de Sant Iu, 5. Tel. 310 58 00. Open from 9 h to 14 h and from 16 h to 19 h. Closed Monday and holiday afternoons. This museum was inaugurated in 1948, thanks to the donation of the collections of Frederic Mares. The museum is set up in a part of the palace of the Monarchs of Aragon. It has an exceptional collection of sculpture on display. One begins with the Iberic votive offerings, Greek terracotta figurines and Roman sculpture. In the basement there are Roman façades and stone sculptures. Climbing upstairs again you find Romanesque sculpture, consisting of crucifixes and Virgens. The Virgen de Plandogau, the Cristo de Taull and a XII century marble relief from Sant Pere de Rodes are outstanding. On the first floor are sculptures from the XV to the XIX centuries; a magnificent collection of alabaster Virgens; and the Polyptico from Calabazanos, with its Santa Clara. Then come good Renaissance and Barroque sculptures and a hall dedicated to works from the XIX century. On the upper floor you find the Museo Sentimental, with a seemingly countless number of objects of personal use from the XVIII and XIX centuries.

Museo Picasso. Montcada, 15. Tel. 315 47 61. Open every day (except Monday, when it is closed) from 10 h to 20 h. Set up in three Gothic-style palaces, in which a progamme of restoration is being carried out. The funds come from Picasso, basically, and his friend Sabartés. The tour begins with the works of Picasso as a child in Málaga and La Coruña, then goes on with the period of his training in Barcelona (1897-1899), with a series of portraits and self-portraits, the best being the *Primera comumión* and *Ciencia y Caridad.*
After a few works that Picasso did in Madrid and in Horta de San Juan, you find his interesting paintings linked with Modernism in Barcelona, and then pass on to his stage in Paris, of which the best are *La Nana* and *Margot.* Between 1902 and 1904 he developed his blue period in Barcelona, with themes featuring social outcasts, which contrast with portraits of his friends and a couple of views of the city. You can see his first sculpture, *Mujer sentada,* from 1902. He returned to Paris in 1905 and began his rose period; the magnificent portrait of the *Señora Canals* belongs to this period. The

collection of this museum is a bit poor in works from Picasso's next stages in painting, the cubist period and later ones, but there is a large collection of graphic work to make up for this lack. The museum has 58 paintings from the exceptional series of *Las Meninas,* from the Mediterranean stage in the decade of the forties.

Fundació Antoni Tapies. Aragó, 255. Tel. 487 03 15. Open Tuesday through Sunday from 11 h to 20 h. Closed Monday. It has a library that specializes in non-western art. The museum has a large collection of the drawings, paintings, sculpture and engravings by Tapies, which provide examples of works from his different periods of evolution, from his primitive paintings of the forties (such as *Zoom* and *Cap i bandera);* to his surrealist period *(Parafaragamus);* to his "Matérica" painting *(Terra i pintura);* his "Objetual" work *(Pintura-bastidor);* to his most recent work. There is no permanent exhibition, but rather, monographic exhibits from the museum's collection are organized to contribute to the particular activity that is being carried out at a given time.

Museo Etnológico. Avinguda Santa Madrona. Parque de Montjuic. Tel. 424 68 07. Open from 9 h to 20.30 h; holidays only from 9 h to 14 h; Monday from 15 h to 20.30 h. It has no permanent exhibition, but rather it organizes periodically changing monographic courses illustrated with material from its large collection. Its collection includes material from Guinea, Gabón, Cameroun, Ethiopia, Morocco, West Africa, textiles from Guatemala, Pre-Colombian American archaeology, ritual and vernacular pieces from Central and South America, pieces from Australia, and good collections from Asia, especially from Japan.

Museo de Cerámica. Avinguda Diagonal, 686. Palacio de Pedralbes. Tel. 205 19 67. Open every day from 9 h to 14 h, except Monday, when it is closed. Medieval Moorish pieces. Major collection from Paterna (XIII and XIV centuries) and Manises (from the XIV century on); outstanding dish *Plato de la Sardana.* Large collection of Catalan pieces; From those of the XVIII century are the groups *La Corrida* and *La Chocolatada.* Collections from Talavera, Alcora, Seville and pieces from XX century artists.

Museo Marítimo. Porta de la Pau, 1. Drassanes Reials (Royal Shipyards). Tel. 301 64 25. Closed Monday; open every other day from 9 h to 14 h, holidays only in the morning. Unique Gothic industrial building. Exhibition of navigational devices, seamen's votive offerings, collection of portolanos (medieval navigation charts), scale models of ships, ship figureheads, and more. Impressive reproduction of the ship of the captain of the Battle of Lepanto ,with a length of 60 metres.

Museo Textil y de la Indumentaria. Montcada 12. Tel. 310 45 16. Closed Monday and holiday afternoon; open every other day from 9 h to 14 h and from 16.30 h to 19 h. Set up in two medieval palaces that have been remodeled at later dates. On the ground floor there are temporary exhibits and a collection of dolls and mannequins (xviii xix centuries). On the main floor there are capes from the xvi century, Barroque women's wear, lavish dresses from the xix century and a collection of Modernist suits; there are also many medieval and Coptic materials.

Museo de la Historia de la Ciudad. Carrer del Verguer. Tel. 315 11 11. Open from 9 h to 20 h; Sunday from 9 h to 13.30 h; Monday from 15 h to 20 h. Set up in a stately home from the xv century which was moved and rebuilt stone by stone in 1931. In the basement you can follow an archaeological itinerary through the Roman city, and see studies of inscriptions and sculptures. On the main floor there is the Roman wall and rooms from the Palau Reial, Chapel and Saló del Tinell.

Museo de la Música. Avinguda de la Diagonal, 373. Tel. 217 11 57. Closed Monday, open every other day from 9 h to 14 h. Modernist mansion built by Puig i Cadafalch in 1902. Extensive collection of every type of musical instrument, illustrating their evolution and characteristics. Extraordinary collection of guitars; Barroque violas by Norman and Tielke; Barroque organs; clavecines by Zell and Flaiser, among others. Wide variety of pianos.

Museo de la Ciencia. Teodor Roviralta, 55. Tel. 212 60 50. Open from 10 h to 20 h. Closed Monday.

Museo del Perfume. Passeig de Gràcia, 39. Tel. 216 01 46. Open from 11 h to 13.30 h and from 17 h to 19.30 h. Closed Saturday afternoon and holidays.

Calendar of fairs and Festivities

January　　*Cavalgada dels Tres Tombs (Parade of Three Rounds)*
In Barcelona on January 17. The Cavalgada parade passes through the Rondas and the San Antonio quar-

ter bearing flags and banners. It is one of the oldest, most tradional fiestas in Barcelona.

Ball del Ciri (The Dance of Candle)

In Manlleu, on January 17. This is a traditional dance of local origin whose origins go back to the XVII century, that is danced in the evening of the feast day of San Antonio.

Baile del Bó-Bó (Dance)

In Monistrol de Montserrat, on January 20. This is a dance for married and single couples, in memory of the terrible epidemic that decimated the population five centuries ago, and which the remainder of the town's citizens survived thanks to the intervention of their patron saint, San Sebastián.

February

Fiesta de la Llum Miraculosa (The Fiesta of the Miraculous Light)

In Manresa, on February 21. This fiesta is celebrated in remembrance of an event that occurred in 1345, thanks to which the citizens of the village could go on with and complete the construction of an irrigation ditch, which had been stopped by order of the Bishop of Vic. That same year the Bishop died, after a strange light coming from Montserrat fell on the altar of the church Iglesia del Carme, and all of the bells of the town began to peal. The work was completed forty years later.

Festa dels Traginers (Fiesta of the Mule Drivers)

In Balsareny, on the Sunday before carnaval. This fiesta has been officially declared to be of Interés Turístico. There is a parade of giants and "big-heads", dancers, horse-back riders, floats and the most lovely of animals, among which is a stud boar. The festivities begin in the morning with the Torrada del Traginer (toasted bread with garlic and wine and anisette); in the afternoon there is a horse race, mule race and ass race. The day finishes off with a dance of Sardanas in the main square.

El Ball de Gitanes (Carnaval)

In Sant Celoni, the capital of the Baix Montseny, the Ball de Gitanes is one of the most outstanding celebrations on the Friday of Carnaval. There was mention of it in documents surviving from the year 1767. The Ball de Gitanes is a very traditional Catalan folkdance. Its name comes from a dance put on by women dressed up as gypsies, and its music is reminiscent of the polca and the waltz.

Festa de l'Arrós (Rice Fiesta)

In San Fruitós de Bages. It is held on the Sunday of Carnaval and usually is a very short time away from the Fiesta Mayor of the winter, in honour of the patron saint San Fructós, which is celebrated on February 21.

Festa de les Comparses (carnaval)

In Villanova i la Geltrú. Its origins go back to the XVIII century, and its moment of climax comes on Carnaval Sunday, when the choral groups dressed in typical costumes parade through the streets singing *Balladas* and *Passades*. There is a costume competition on Saturday night. The character of *El Carnestoles* is in charge of reading the ryhmes which ironically poke fun at the people of the cummunity.

Carnaval in the City of Barcelona

The festivities last from Thursday to Tuesday, and are opened with a speech by the Carnestoles. During the weekend they put on the Rua, which consists of a parade of floats along the Paralelo. The children go to the parks with a mackerel hanging from a fishing pole and they bury it there.

Mercat del Ram (Market)

In Vic, on the Saturday before Palm Sunday. This is a traditional market that is held in the main square, and has been declared of Interés Turístico. Palm leaves, *palmones* and rosemary are on sale, to be taken to the procession of *Los Armados,* or used to decorate the houses during the fiestas. In the afternoon there is a procession, in which those who have to keep some promise participate, preceded by a group of Romans.

March

Romería de Sant Medir (Romería of San Emeterio)

In San Cugat del Vallès, on March 3. The origin of the festivities organized around this procession are involved with the vow of the baker Josep Vidal, who in 1830 promised to make a pilgrimage to the hermitage located in the Valle de Gausac if San Medir cured him of a serious illness. That pilgrimage has grown to a group of pilgrims today, who with their *abanderado* and *cordonistas* continue with what has become a tradition involving a picnic at the hermitage.

Holy Week
La Passió

In Esparraguera, this fiesta has been declared of Interés Turístico, with a Passion play put on every Sunday in March and April (except the week of the Resurrection, when it is enacted on Good Friday) and May 1. Its origins go back to the XVII century and require the participation of 100 actors. The text was written by Ramón Torruella i Satorra and is divided into two parts, the *Public Life of Jesus* and the *Passion, Death and Resurrection*. The *Teatro de la Passió* was inaugurated in 1969, to be used as the venue for the play.

La Passió

In Olesa de Montserrat, on Sundays and holidays in Lent and during Holy Week. The *Passió* of Olesa was mentioned in documents from 1642. It is enacted in the *Gran Teatre de la Passió.*

Auto Sacramental de la Passió

In Sant Vincent dels Horts they have been enacting Good Friday afternoon for the last four centuries in the parish church.

April

Fiesta Patronal de la Virgen de Montserrat

In the Monastery of Montserrat, on April 27. In the evening they celebrate the Vetla de Santa María. On the feast day of the Virgen there is an extraordinary liturgical ceremony, with a special Mass and singing of vespers.

Fiesta de Sant Jordi

In Barcelona on April 23. Officially declared of Interés Turístico. The city fills up with stalls where books and roses are sold, to be used as gifts on this day. Beforehand there is the visit, traditional since the xv century, to the chapel of the saint in the Generalitat building.

May

Fira de Sant Ponç

In the city of Barcelona, on May 11. There is the exhibit and sale of aromatic and medicinal herbs in stalls set up on the Calle del Hospital during the Feria of Sant Ponç, the patron saint of homeopaths.

Fiestas de la Ascensión

In Granollers, this one usually lasts from Wednesday to Sunday. The festivities are celebrated in the area of the Mercat.

June

Aplec de la Sardana

In Calella, on the first Sunday in June. This fiesta has been declared of Interés Turístico, and has been held since 1927. Four or five *cobles* dance the Sardanas.

Corpus Cristi
La Patum

In Berga; declared of Interés Turístico. It is held on the evening of the Thursday of Corpus Christi and the following Sunday; the night before there is a traditional procession to the beat of drums played by El Tabaler, and there are the four Giants. In the afternoon there is the traditional performance of *La Patum* in the streets and squares. On the day of the fiesta (both on Thursday and on Sunday) there is another *Patum,* after the Mass is said. The eagle represents royal power and the liberation of the village from the feudal lords, linked to the origin of the fiesta, which is none other than the incorporation of Berga into the Crown of King Juan I, "the hunter", in 1393.

Festes del Carrer

In Capellades, on the eighth of Corpus Christi, the citizens divide themselves in five quarters, to celebrate the fiesta on different days. The celebration begins with parades to music, then there is the blessing of the *tortells* (sweets) which are then distributed by the organizers in each quarter to the respective families.

Enramades
In Sallent, the origin of this fiesta goes back to a legend about the people of this community and how they escaped from a blood-thirsty army by camouflaging themselves with thick bunches of branches.

Festa dels Barris
In San Sadurní d'Anoia, this fiesta is organized for the day after Corpus Christi, and lasts until the following Tuesday. The town is divided into seven neighbourhoods, and four male and two female administrators are named in each. There is a dance of Sardanas the night before.

Concurso de Alfombras de Flores (Flower Carpet Competition)
In Sitges, declared of Interés Turístico. This is probably the competition that draws the largest crowds in all of Catalonia.

Coca de Sant Joan
In Barcelona, on June 23. The *coca* is the typical sweet of this fiesta. Outdoor dancing and bonfires are organized in all the neighbourhoods.

Festa dels Pescadors
In Vilanova i la Geltrú, on June 29. There is a parade of boats carrying the statue of Sant Pere. The statue rides in a boat bedecked with wreathes which leads the procession of boats which are also decorated, and which all receive the priest's blessing. The night before there is a competition of *All Cremat* (toasted garlic), a typical dish prepared by the fishermen.

Fiestas de Primavera
In Torelló, usually on the feast of Corpus Christi, although sometimes on any other day in the month of June.

July

Festes de Sant Miquel dels Sants
In Vic, around July 5. The fiesta lasts 10 days. The relics of the saint are taken from the house he was born in, to the Cathedral, and there are fireworks, parades of giants and "big-heads", dancing of Sardanas and *Tornaboda de la Festa Major,* with dancing and eating of sausages and the Catalan version of the pizza, the coca.

Festa Major in honour of the Saints Juliana and Semproniana
In Mataró the fiesta celebrations are from July 25-29. The most outstanding performance is that of the *Oficio de las Santas,* performed by an orchestra and mixed choir. In addition there is a Festival de Cante Flamenco, symphonic concerts, music bands and *grallers,*

singing of *habaneras, ballada de Sardanes,* giants and "big-heads", *castellers* and the distribution of *El Cremat* from Les Santes.

Festa del Elois

In Berga, on the last Sunday in July. The fiesta is in honour of the patron saint of the mule drivers.

Festa Major of the Saints Abdón and Senén

In Pla de Penedès, on the last Saturday in July. They perform the dances of the *dimonis, els bastoners, el drac, els cercolets,* and there are recitals and Sardana competitions.

August

Fiesta del Cántaro

In Argentona, on August 4. This feast day of Santo Domingo is celebrated by the buying and selling of thousands of earthenware pitchers. In the *Xabotada del Cantín,* the children demonstrate their strength and skill in games related with objects of pottery. Beforehand there are pottery exhibitions all over Catalonia.

Festa Major de San Félix

In Vilafranca del Penedès, from mid-day on August 29 until August 31. There is a get-together of *colles de castelers,* who put up their imposing human towers in the village's main square, in front of the Ayuntamiento. On the afternoon of the saint's feast day everyone joins the procession behind the statue of San Félix to the Basilica.

September

La Diada nacional

On September 11 they celebrate the day of Catalonia.

Festa Major in honour of Nuestra Señora del Patrimonio

In Cardona, on the second Sunday in September. During the fiesta there is the *Corre del Bou (Running of the Bull),* considered to be the oldest bull-fighting show in Spain, and declared of Interés Turístico. A man stands in front of the bull, protected by nothing more than a wicker basket called the *cargolera,* and from which only his feet and head stick out. The fellow gets the bull to charge, and when it attempts to gore him, he takes hold of some handles inside while pulling in his extremities, while the bull sends the man in the basket rolling about.

Festas de la Mercé

In Barcelona, September 22-24. The Fiestas de la Mercé were set up to give the city a patron saint fiesta, something which it had lacked. Although the Virgen has been the patron saint since the XVII century, it was not until the last century that the capital of Catalonia began to dedicate these festivities in honour of its patron. These completely urban fiestas are linked to rural events. According to legend there was a terrible plague of locusts which was eating up all the crops in the year 1867. After they had tried everything else in their battle against the scourge, the country peasants turned to their religious beliefs, and decided to name the Virgen de la Mercé the patron saint and protector of Barcelona. The next year there was no plague at all. Thus having demonstrated her effectiveness, the Virgen de la Mercé was fully accepted as the patron saint of the city, and for many of the local country people she will go on being the *Mother of God of the locusts*. The most traditional events are the performances of the *gegants* and the *correfocs*. The latter are fireworks displays in which the participation of the spectators forms an integral part. The dancers carry torches, sparklers and firecrackers through the crowd, and the mixture of smoke, fire and noise with the motion of the people causes a stunning effect. The *Colles de Castellers* build impresively high human towers. You hear the traditional Habanera songs and see the Sardana dances everywhere. If you like to eat well, you will be able to sample typical Catalan dishes in the Muestra de Cocina Barcelonesa which takes place on the Avenida Gaudí.

October

Concurso de Setas (Mushroom Competition)
In Berga, on October 5. The *boletaires* spend this day looking for mushrooms, to compete in this contest held each year.

November

Festa de la Catanyada (Chestnut)
In Perafita, on All Saints night, the people of the village get together in the Plaza Mayor to light a giant bonfire, over which they roast salted mackerel, chestnuts and the Catalan version of the pizza, the coca.

December

Fira de Sant Llúcia
In Barcelona, on December 13. The Fair is set up a few days ahead in front of the Cathedral and in the Plaza de la Sagrada Familia, featuring Nativity scenes. On December 13 many devout people visit the chapel Capilla de la Santa Llúcia in the Cathedral.
Pesebre Viviente (Living Manger)
In Corbera de Llobregat, on Chrismas Eve and Christmas Day. The people of the village bring their Nativity Scene to life by portraying the main scenes related with the birth of Christ.
Festa del Pi (Fiesta of teh Pine)
In Centelles, on December 30. The fiesta starts at dawn when the *galejadors* and *trabucaires* fire their weapons unitl they run out of powder. Groups of men dressed in typical costumes go to the mountain to collect a previously selected pine tree. Before returning

with the tree, they light bonfires and roast "butifarras" (sausage). The pine is put up in the main square, the *galejadors* join in a circle around it to make even more noise. Afterwards the tree is brought into the church, where it remains until January 6. On that day its branches are shared out among the faithful while they sing the *Himno de Santa Coloma,* whose *festa major d'hivern (winter patron saint fiesta) is celebrated the following day.*

Shows and Entertainment

Theatres

Gran Teatro del Liceu. Opera season from November to June. There is the occasional show in the off season. The theatre is the headquarters of the Orquesta Sinfónica and Coro del Gran Teatro del Liceu. Carrer Sant Pau, 1. Tel. 318 92 77 and Rambla des Caputxins, 66. Tel. 412 35 32.

Jove Teatro Regina. Séneca, 22. Tel. 218 15 12. There is a programme for adults during the week and for children on Saturday afternoon and Sunday morning.

Mercat de les Flors. Carrer Lleida, 59. Tel. 426 18 75. Box-offices: Palau de la Virreina, Rambla, 99. Tel. 318 10 83. Ajuntament de Barcelona.

Sala Beckett. Alegre del Dalt, 55 bis (Gràcia). Tel. 219 79 27.

Lluire. Montseny, 47 (Gràcia). Tel. 218 92 51.

Teatre Malic. Fussina, 3. Tel. 310 70 35.

Poliorama. Rambles dels Estudis, 115. The seat of the Teatre Catala de la Comedia. Tel. 317 75 99.

Romea. Hospital, 51. Tel. 317 71 89. Seat of the Centre Dramatic de la Generalitat de Catalunya.

Victoria. Paralel, 67. They put on grand music and variety shows.

Villarroel Teatre. Villarroel, 87 (Eixample). Tel. 451 12 34.

Festivals

Theatre

El Grec de Barcelona. Palau de la Virreina, Rambla, 99. Tel. 302 77 52. A variety of daily shows involving theatre, dance, cinema, music and song, from the end of June to the middle of August. Most of the work is put on in the Teatre Grec on Montjuïc, in the open air, although they also use other venues. At the same time is the Festival de Flamenco and the Semana Internacional de Cine in Barcelona.

Festival Internacional de Teatro in Sitges. From the end of April to the first part of May. Patronato del Festival, Plaça de l'Ajuntament, 18. Tel. 894 45 61.

Over a ten-day period, roughly, one can select from some thirty shows staged by major Spanish and foreign companies.

Cinema
Festival Internacional de Cine Fantástico y de Terror (Fantas-Film). In Sitges, in October. There is an official judging of films, and films shown outside of the competition, along with the presence of famous directors and actors, film series, video, and more. Information: Diputación, 279. Tel. 317 35 85.

Shopping

Gastronomy

Pastry
Baixas. Calaf, 9. Its "tarta de Sacher" is excellent, as are its *apfel strudel* and *plumcake.*

Escribá. Gran Vía, 546. A classic shop, especially with its Easter season selection. Specializes in chocolate, "cocas" de San Juan, Roscón de Reyes and *panellets.*

Fargo. Diagonal, 391. Closed Sunday afternoon. Sherbets and ice cream made on the premises. Homemade pastry, agreeable tea room.

Foix de Sarrià. Plaza de Sarrià, 9 and Major de Sarrià, 57. Founded in 1886. Excellent bonbons, biscuits and *panellets.* Has *petxinas* on sale between September and May.

Fontanet. Mare de Deu del Coll, 1. Excellent pastries, "cocas", "buñuelos de viento", *panellets.*

Mauri. Rambla de Cataluna, 102 and Provença, 241. Closed Sunday afternoon. Large selection of high quality pastry, plus a tea room.

Mora. Diagonal, 409. It has a bar and four tables, specializing in biscuits, pastries and bonbons, and especially in the *Tronc de Nadal.*

Richart. Muntaner, 463. Over 80 different types of filled bonbons. A branch of the Parisian bonbon makers.

Wines and Liqueurs
Augusta. Vía Augusta, 8. All kinds of wines, as well as cavas, champagnes and liqueurs.

Celler de Gelida. Vallespir, 65. Tel. 339 26 41. Catalan wines, and from Rioja and Rueda, as well as liqueurs, cavas, and armagnacs.

Colmado Murrià. Roger de Llúria, 85. In addition to its cava de Murrià, orange wine, "worm" liqueur and other curiosities, it has a good selection of Catalan and Rioja wines, and above all, a good delicatessen.

José Melendo. Santaló, 41. Tel. 200 65 38. A stupendous selection of wines.

Lafuente. Juan Sebastián Bach, 20. It has all kinds of wines and liqueurs.

La Barcelonina de Vins i Espirits. Valencia, 304. A stock of more than 400 kinds of wine, with experts ready to give their advice. Also sells books.

Handicrafts

In Barcelona the handicraft fair par excellance is El Poble Espayol de Montjuic, where craftsmen work before spectators and offer their wares for sale. Nevertheless, you can find handicraft shops in the old quarter too, generally in the same part of the *call* where the antique shops are. The Generalitat de Cataluña runs a Centro Permanente de Artesanía on Paseo de Gràcia, 55. Vernacular art and handicrafts are on display there, and in addition it provides information about all kinds of handicraft products.

Antiques

The antique dealers are concentrated in very well-defined areas in Barcelona, the largest of them being in the neighbourhood of the church Iglesia del Pi, on the Calle Sant Domènec del Call, Calle de la Palla, Banys Nous, Petrixol, Avinyó, and Plaza de Sant Josep Oriol. Another area of antique shops is the one on Paseo Gràcia-Rambla de Catalunya.

Mercat Gotic. Every Thursday a large group of antique dealers sets up a fair in the Plaza del Pi.

Centre d'Antiquaris. Paseo de Gràcia, 57.

Los Encants Nous (Fira de Bellcaire). This is the flea market in Barcelona, and has a long tradition of offering bargains and rarities. Open every Monday, Wednesday, Friday and Saturday in the Plaza de las Glories Catalanes, tel. 246 30 30. Open from 8 h until dark.

Centro Comercial Encantos Nuevos. Valencia, 534.

Encants Vells-Mercat de San Antoni. They sell articles of clothing in the market of San antoni. Open Monday, Wednesday, Friday and Saturday. On Sunday in the same spot there is a little market where you can find second-hand magazines, photographs, press clippings, and more.

Mercadillo Filatélico y Numismático de la Plaza Real. Held on Sunday mornings in the Plaza Real, beside the lower part of the Ramblas. Stamps and coins from all over the world are sold and exchanged, as well as albums and catalogues.

Mercadillos de arte

Plaza de Josep Oriol. Open Saturday and Sunday morning. Painters display their works in the open air, selling them directly to the public.

Feria de Nueva Artesanía
Rambla de Santa Mònica. Tel. 318 93 12. Open Saturday and Sunday, from the morning until dark.

What to do with the Kids

Golondrinos
These little boats go from the harbour (in front of the Monument to Columbus) to the breakwater. Although the used to be a little kitsch, they have become an appealing tourist attraction. Information and reservations, Señor Cristóbal, tel. 302 52 24.

Tibidabo (Amusement Park)
A great viewpoint some 500 m above sea level. You can climb up in your car on the Carretera de l'Arrabassada, or take the *tranvia blau*, the last one in Barcelona. You can catch it at the Tibidabo underground station. Tel. 417 03 38.

Parque de Atracciones de Montjuïc
Tel. 441 70 24 and 442 31 75. City bus number 61 from the Plaza de España. Open Saturdays, Sundays and holidays from 12 h to 20 h.

Catalunya en Miniatura
In Torrelles de Llobregat, 17 km from Barcelona. This Theme Park has been declared of Interés Turístico Nacional, with more than 170 monuments in miniature from all over Catalonia. Information, tel. 689 09 60.

Zoo de Barcelona
In the Parque de la Ciudadela. Tel. 309 25 00. Open from 10 h to 19 h.

Acuario de Barcelona
Paseo Nacional. Barceloneta. Tel. 319 43 28.

Skating
Roger de Flor, 168. Tel. 245 28 00. Closed Monday.

Malgrat de Mar
Marineland
Palafolls-Malgrat de Mar, km 2.7. Tel. 761 28 02.

Sitges
Aquátic Paradis (Aquatic Park)
Mas del Pins. Tel. 894 03 69.

Addresses and Helpul hints

If you would like to telephone any of the organisms or establishments cited below while outside of the Province of Barcelona, you must first dial the code number 93.

HOTELS

Ritz H*****GL
Gran Vía, 668.
Tel. 318 52 00.
Avenida Palace H*****
Gran Vía, 605. Tel. 301 96 00.
Diplomatic H*****
Pau Claris, 122.
Tel. 317 31 00.
Meliá Barcelona Sarria H*****
Avenida Sarria, 50.
Tel. 410 60 60.
President H*****
Avinguda Diagonal, 570.
Tel. 200 21 11.
Princesa Sofía H*****
Plaza Papa Pío XII, 4.
Tel. 330 71 11.
Ramada Renaissance Barcelona H*****
Ramblas, 111. Tel. 318 62 00.
Suite Hotel H*****
Muntaner, 505. Tel. 212 80 12.
Alexander H****
Mallorca, 251. Tel. 487 05 05.
Arenas HR****
Capitán Arenas, 20.
Tel. 280 03 03.
Balmoral HR****
Vía Augusta, 5. Tel. 217 87 00.
Barcelona HR****
Caspe, 1. Tel. 302 58 58.

Colón H****
Avinguda Catedral, 7.
Tel. 301 14 04.
Condes de Barcelona H****
Paseo de Gracia, 75. Tel. 487 37 37.
Cristal HR****
Diputaión, 257. Tel. 301 66 00.
Cóndor HR****
Vía Augusta, 127. Tel. 209 45 11.
Dante HR****
allorca, 181. Tel. 323 22 54.
Derby HR****
Loreto, 21. Tel. 322 32 15.
Duques de Bergara H****
Bergara, 11. Tel. 301 51 51.
Europark HR****
Aragón, 325. Tel. 257 92 05.
Gran Derby HA****
Loreto, 28. Tel. 322 32 15.
Gran Hotel Calderón HR****
Rambla de Cataluña, 26.
Tel. 301 00 00.
Gran Hotel Cristina HR****
Avinguda de la Diagonal, 458.
Tel. 217 68 00.
Hesperia HR****
Los Vergos, 20. Tel. 204 55 51.
Majestic H****
Paseo de Gracia, 70.
Tel. 215 45 12.
Master H****
Valencia, 105. Tel. 423 62 15.
Núñez-Urgel HR****
Urgel, 232. Tel. 322 41 53.
Park Putxet H****
Putxet, 68-74.
Tel. 212 51 58.
Rekord HA****
Muntaner, 352.
Tel. 200 19 53.

Regent H****
Rambla de Cataluña, 76.
Tel. 215 25 70.
Rivoli Ramblas H****
Rambla dels Estudis, 128.
Tel. 302 66 43.
Roma H****
Avinguda de Roma, 31.
Tel. 410 66 33.
Royal HR****
Ramblas, 117.
Tel. 310 94 00.
Victoria RA****
Avinguda Pedralbes, N.16.
Tel. 204 27 54.
Aragón HR***
Aragón, 569. Bis 571.
Tel. 245 89 05.
Astoria HR***
Paris, 203. Tel. 209 83 11.
Augusta RA***
Lincoln, 32. Tel. 218 33 55.
Balmes H***
Mallorca, 216. Tel. 451 19 14.
Belagua H***
Vía Augusta, 89.
Tel. 237 39 40.
Beltrán HA***
Beltrán, 150. Tel. 212 75 50.
Condado H***
Aribau, 210. Tel. 200 23 11.
Covadonga HR***
Avinguda Diagonal, 596.
Tel. 209 55 11.
Expo Hotel HR***
Mallorca, 1 to 23.
Tel. 325 12 12.
Ficus HR***
Mallorca, 163. Tel. 353 35 00.
Gala Placida HA***
Via Augustus, 112. Tel. 217 82 00.
Gran Vía H***
Gran Vía Corts Catalanes, 642.
Tel. 318 19 00.
Gravina H***
Gravina, 12. Tel. 301 68 68.
Gótico HR***
Jaime I, 14. Tel. 315 22 11.
Habana HR***
Gran Vía, 647. Tel. 301 07 50.
Metropol H***
Ample, 31. Tel. 315 40 11.

Mikado HA***
P. de la Bonanova, 58.
Tel. 211 41 66.
Mitre HR***
Beltrán, 9 and 15. Tel. 212 11 04.
Moderno H***
Hospital, 11. Tel. 301 41 54.
Montecarlo HR***
Rambla dels Estudis, 124.
Tel. 317 58 00.
NH Les Corts HR***
Travessera de las Corts, 292.
Tel. 322 08 11.
Numancia HR***
Numancia, 74. Tel. 322 44 51.
Oriente H***
Ramblas, 45 and 47. Tel. 302 25 58.
Pedralbes H***
Fontcoberta, 4. Tel. 203 71 12.
Rallye HR***
Travessera de las Corts, 150.
Tel. 339 90 50.
Regencia Colón HR***
Sagristans, 13 to 17.
Tel. 318 98 58.
Regina H***
Bergara, 2. Tel. 301 32 32.
Rialto HR***
Carrer Ferran, 40 and 42.
Tel. 318 52 12.
Rubens HA***
Nuestra Señora del Coll, 10.
Tel. 219 12 04.
Suizo H***
Plaza del Ángel, 12. Tel. 315 41 11.
Taber HR***
Aragón, 256. Tel. 318 70 50.
Terminal HR***
Provenza, 1. Tel. 321 53 50.
Tres Torres HR***
Calatrava, 32 and 34.
Tel. 417 73 00.
Turín H***
Pintor Fortuny, 9. Tel. 302 48 12.
Villa de Madrid HR***
Plaza Villa de Madrid, 3.
Tel. 317 49 16.
Wilson HR***
Diagonal, 568. Tel. 209 25 11.
Zenit HR***
Santalo, 8.
Tel. 209 89 11.

In Montseny
San Bernat H***
Finca del Cot. Tel. 847 30 11.

In Montserrat
Abad Cisneros H***
Plaça de Montserrat. Tel. 835 02 01.
Monasterio HSR***
Plaça Monestir. Tel. 835 02 01.
Colonia Puig H*
Carretera Monistrol-Montserrat.
Tel. 835 02 68.

In Sitges
Antemare H****
Verge Montserrat, 48-50.
Tel. 894 70 00.
Caliopolis HR****
Paseo Marítimo.
Tel. 894 15 00.
Mediterraneo HA****
Avenida Sofía, 3.
Tel. 894 51 34.
San Sebastián Playa H****
Port Alegre, 53.
Subur Marítim H****
Puerto Marítimo. Tel. 894 15 50.
Terramar HR****
Passeig Marítim, 30. Tel. 894 00 50.
Galeón HR***
San Francisco, 44-46. Tel. 894 06 12.

PARADOR HOTELS

Parador Duques de Cardona**
Cardona (Barcelona)
Tel. 869 12 75. Fax. 869 16 36.
This Parador is located inside a
fortress which Luis de Aquitania
began to have built in 798. One of
the main buildings within the
fortress is the Church of San Vicente,
the finest example of the original
Romanesque-Lombard style of architecture of the XI century.

Parador de Vich**
Vich (Barcelona). Tel. 888 72 11.
Fax. 888 73 11.
Built in the style of the country
manor houses of Catalonia.

HOT SPRINGS RESORTS

Blancafort**
In La Garriga, 10 km from Granollers
and 36 km from Barcelona.
Tel. 871 46 00.
Fax. 871 57 50.
Hot springs resort open all year
round. Therapeutic treatment of res-
piratory system problems, rheuma-
tism and traumatology, nervous and
blood circulatory system problems,
stress, skin disorders and obesity.
Broquetas**
In Caldas de Montbuy (Barcelona),
28 km from Barcelona.
Tel. 865 01 00. Fax. 865 23 12.
Open all year round. Therapy for
rheumatism and traumatology, respiratory, nervous and blood circulatory system problems, obesity.
Termas Victoria**
In Caldas de Montbuy (Barcelona)
Tel. 865 01 50. Fax. 865 08 16.
Open all year round. Therapy for respiratory, nervous and blood circulation system disorders, rheumatism,
traumatology and obesity.
Termas de Salud*
In Caldas de Montbuy (Barcelona),
17 km from Sabadell and 28 km
from Barcelona. Tel. 865 00 98.
Open from May 1 to October 31.
Therapy for Rheumatism, traumatology, obesity and nervous system disorders.
Termas Sola*
In Caldas de Montbuy (Barcelona),
near Sabadell, Granollers and Barcelona.
Tel. 865 00 95.
Therapy for respiratory, nervous and
blood circulation system disorders,
and traumatology.

Forns
In Caldas de Montbuy (Barcelona),
28 km from Barcelona.
Tel. 865 00 85/11 50.
Open all year round.
Therapy for rheumatism, traumatol-
ogy and nervous system disorders.

CAMPGROUNDS

La Ballena Alegre. First category. Viladecans, Castelldefels motorway, km 12.5. Tel. 658 05 04. Open from May 15 to September 30.

Filipinas. First category. Viladecans, Castelldefels motorway, km 12. Tel. 658 28 95. Open all year round.

El Toro Bravo. First category. Viladecans, Castelldefels motorway, km 12. Tel. 637 34 62.

Cala-Gogo-El Prat. First category. Prat de Llobregat. Tel. 379 46 00. Open from February 1 to November 30. Lots of different kinds of trees, a lot of shade, sandy beach.

Albatross. First category. Gavá, Castelldefels motorway, km 15. Tel. 662 20 31. Open from May 27 through September. Heated pool.

La Tortuga Alegre. First category. Gavá. Bertrand y Musitu, 69. Tel. 662 12 29. Open all year round.

Tres Estrellas. First category. Gavá. Castelldefels motorway, km 13.2. Tel. 662 11 16. Open from April 1 to September 30.

Estrella de Mar. Second Category. Castelldefels, Castelldefels motorway, km 16.7. Tel. 665 32 57. Open all year round.

Masia Can Cervera. Third category. Montseny, Palau-Tordera-Collformic highway, km 15. Tel. 847 30 66. Open from January 15 to December 15.

Vilanova Park. First category. Vilanova i la Geltrú, L'Arboc highway, km 2.5. Tel. 893 34 02. Open all year round.

Platja Vilanova. Second category. Vilanova i Geltrú, C 246 highway, km 48. Open from April 1 to September 30.

Los Almendros. Second category. Sitges, Camí Capellans, 32. Tel. 894 09 49. Open from March 17 to September 30.

Garraf. Second category. Sitges, Barcelona-Santa Cruz Calafell highway, km 25. Open from April 1 to September 10.

El Garrofel. Second category. Sitges, C 246 highway, km 39. At a distance of 2 km from the centre of Sitges, one km from the beach. Tel. 894 17 80. Open all year round.

El Roca. Second category. Sitges, Sitges-San Pere de Ribes highway. Tel. 894 00 43. Open from March 1 to September 30. It is located on a height of land with a beautiful panoramic view of Sitges and the sea. Long sandy beach one km away.

Sitges. Second category. Sitges, C 246 highway, km 38. Tel. 894 10 80. Open from March 1 to October 15.

Sol. Second category. Sitges. Vallpineda-Sitges highway. Tel. 894 22 44. Open from January 15 to Decmber 15.

Club las salinas. First category. Cubells, C 246 highway, km 51. Tel. 895 10 00. Open from January 15 to December 15.

La Rueda. First category. Cubellas, C 246 highway, km 52.1. Tel. 895 02 07. Open from March 23 to September 24. Located between the seaside, the country and the residencial zones. Sandy beach.

El Vedado. First category. Vallromanas, Masnou-Granollers highway, km 7. Tel. 568 13 92. Open from January 15 to December 15. Located in a valley surrounded by mountains, with pine and holm oak woods.

Repós de Pedraforca. First category. Saldés, B 400 highway, km 13.5. Tel. 822 75 34. Open all year round. Located in beautiful natural surroundings, across from Pedraforca and the Parque Natural Cadí-Moixero.

El Paradiso. Second category. Cubellas, Avenida de la Pineda. Tel. 895 04 89. Open from March 15 to September 30.

Barcino. Second category. Esplugas de Llobregat. Laureano Miró, 50. N II highway, km 616. Tel. 372 85 01. Open all year round.

Kanguro. Second category. San Pol de Mar, N II highway, km 661.5. Tel. 760 02 05. Open from April 1 to September 15.

La Maresme. Second category. San Pol de Mar, San Cebriá highway. Tel. 760 03 56. Open from April 1 to September 30. Banana plantation, very shady. Sandy beach.

MEANS OF TRANSPORT

Aeropuerto Internacional de Barcelona in El Prat de Llobregat, 15 km to the southeast of Barcelona. Tel. 317 86 08 and 379 24 54. Flight information tel. 325 43 04. Transport from the airport to the city by bus, train, taxi.

Aeropuerto de Sabadell
Tel. 710 16 40.
Iberia: Paseo de Gracia, 30. Diputación, 258. National flight reservations:
Tel. 301 68 00.
International flight reservations:
302 76 56.
Freight reservations:
Tel. 370 40 12.
Inforiberia (information):
Tel. 301 39 93.

Railway
Ferrocarriles de la Generalitat:
Tel. 205 15 15.
R.E.N.F.E. (Information):
Tel. 490 04 80.
Railway station: Central-Sants, Plaça Paisos Catalnas:
Tel. 322 41 41.
De França, Avinguda del Marques del'Argentara:
Tel. 319 32 00.

Compañia Transmediterránea
For the Balearic and Canary Islands
Vía Laietana, 2. Tel. 310 25 08.

For Génova and North Africa
Vía Laietana, 7.
Puerto Autónomo de Barcelona (Harbour)
Information. Tel. 318 87 50.
Pier for the Balearic Islands: Moll de Barcelona. Tel. 317 80 87.
Pier for international service: Moll de Ponent. Tel. 301 25 98.

City Transport
Metropolitano (information for the underground): Tel. 237 45 45.
Buses: Ronda de Santa Pau, 43. Tel. 241 28 00.
Transportes Publicos Urbanos (information): Tel. 336 00 00.

Taxis
Radiotaxis:
Tel. 330 38 11 /322 22 22/ 330 08 04.
Tele Ruta: Highway conditions.
Tel. 204 22 47.

CAR RENTALS

Avis. Airport: Tel. 379 40 26.
Pedro IV, 235. Tel. 308 99 99.
Casanova, 209. Tel. 209 95 33.
Aragón, 235. Tel. 215 84 30.
Rita Bonnat, 5. Tel. 322 77 77.
Europa, 34-36. Tel. 419 64 96.

Europcar. Aeropuerto del Prat:
Tel. 379 90 51.
Consejo del Ciento, 363.
Tel. 317 58 76.
Viladomat, 214. Tel. 439 84 01.
Hotel Princesa sofía.
Plaza Pío XII, 4. Tel. 330 63 58.

Hertz. Aeropuerto del Prat:
Tel. 370 58 11.
Tuset, 10. Tel. 217 80 76.
Estación de Ferrocarril (Sants).
Tel. 490 86 62.

Budget. Avinguda de Roma, 15.
Tel. 322 90 12.
Extremadura, 13.
Tel. 661 51 58.

Sant Boi de Llobregat.
Tel. 630 40 79.

NEWSPAPERS

La Vanguardia
Pelayo, 28. Tel. 301 54 54.
El Periodico de Catalunya. comte
d'Urgel, 71-73. Tel. 451 32 32.

TOURIST INFORMATION

Barcelona
Plaça de Neruda. Tel. 245 76 21.
Estacción de França.
Tel. 319 25 91.
Estación de Sants.
Tel. 250 25 94.
**Oficina de Información
de Turismo**
Gran Vía de les Corts Catalanes,
658. Tel. 301 74 43.
Oficina Municipal de Turismo
Plaça de Sant Jaume.
Tel. 318 25 25.

Arenys de Mar
Passeig de Xifré.
Tel. 792 15 37.

Calella
Sant Jaume.
Tel. 769 05 59.

Castelldefels
Plaça de la Rosa dels Vents.
Tel. 664 23 01.

Sitges
Plaça d'Eduard Maristany.
Tel. 894 12 30.

Vilanova i la Geltrú
Plaça de la Vila,8.
Tel. 893 00 00.

POST OFFICE (CORREOS)
Plaça d'Antoni López.
Tel. 318 38 31.

TELEGRAPH AND TELEX

EL CORREO
International telegrams: Ronda de
Sant Pere, 9.
Tel. 317 91 96.

TELEPHONES (TELEFONOS)
Fontanella, 4.

Index